# Reef Fishes
## of the
# Indian Ocean

# Reef Fishes
## of the
# Indian Ocean

*A pictorial guide to the
common reef fishes
of the Indian Ocean*

**by Gerald R. Allen
and Roger C. Steene**

All photos by the authors

# TABLE OF CONTENTS

We dedicate this book to John E. Randall, Curator of Ichthyology at the Bernice P. Bishop Museum, Honolulu, Hawaii. His knowledge of coral reef fishes and prodigious number of publications on this subject are legendary. "Jack" continues to be an inspiration and inexhaustible fountain of knowledge to divers, students, and professional ichthyologists the world over.

# ABOUT THE AUTHORS

**DR. GERALD R. ALLEN** is a recognized authority on the classification of tropical Indo-Pacific reef fishes and the freshwater fishes of the Australia-New Guinea region. He has written six books and over 70 scientific papers dealing with these subjects and has traveled to over 40 countries, spending hundreds of hours underwater in quest of scientific specimens and close-up photographs of tropical reef fishes. Dr. Allen resides in Perth, where he is Curator of Fishes at the Western Australian Museum.

**ROGER C. STEENE** was born in Australia and lives at Cairns on the Great Barrier Reef. He is an associate of both the Australian Museum, Sydney, and the Western Australian Museum, Perth, and is recognized internationally as a leading underwater photographer and naturalist. He has dived and photographed at numerous localities in the Pacific and Indian Oceans.

**Note:** Some of the photographs featured in this book were taken outside the Indian Ocean, primarily on the Great Barrier Reef of Australia or at New Britain in Melanesia. Without exception the species illustrated in these photographs also occur in the Indian Ocean. The extralimital illustrations were substituted in favor of those taken in the Indian Ocean because of their superior quality.

# Preface

The major islands of the Indian Ocean and continental areas bordering its margins have been known to Arabian and European navigators for centuries. Sleek Arab dhows plied this great ocean eastward to the Maldives and Sri Lanka as early as the 12th century. The last "Golden Age" of exploration and discovery is now well over a century behind us. It seems ironic that today it is possible to traverse this ocean by commercial jetliner in only 10 hours, a trip that 100 years ago required weeks, not to mention the risk to life and limb. The arrival of mass jet travel and concurrent development of SCUBA diving equipment have fostered another, equally exciting, age of discovery. Today a new breed of explorer, the diving scientist and underwater photographer, is able to reach nearly any destination quickly and efficiently and soon after arrival can explore previously unseen terrain below the sea's surface. Scores of exciting fishes, formerly undetected, are being discovered on Indian Ocean reefs by a relatively small band of scientific and photographic pioneers. It is a genuine thrill to play a part in this new era of exploration.

We began work on this book during March, 1978, with a trip to Western Australia, site of some of the world's southernmost coral reefs. Fourteen months and 65,000 km later we had gathered the necessary photos for this book. Our travels took us along the West Australian coast between the Recherche Archipelago and Abrolhos Islands, to remote Christmas Island, Phuket and the Similan Islands of Thailand, Sri Lanka, the Maldive Islands, the Seychelles, Mauritius, Kenya, and South Africa. To round out the coverage we have included a number of photos from the Red Sea and Gulf of Oman taken during 1977. During these travels we collectively shot 12,312 photographs and spent some 650 man-hours under the sea. We also utilized slides from our combined Pacific collections when substitutions were necessary.

*Reef Fishes of the Indian Ocean* represents the results of these efforts. This is not the standard coffee table book of pretty fish pictures representing a particular photographer's collection of best photos. Although many of our photos are esthetically artistic, the main concern is to present a collection that will give the reader a true appreciation of the great diversity of fish life found in the Indian Ocean. Therefore, this volume will also serve as a valuable field guide due to the comprehensive coverage. With it the user will be able to recognize the majority of common fishes found on Indian Ocean reefs. We have made an effort to satisfy the needs of all interested parties . . . whether they be aquarists, divers, scientists, or armchair naturalists. We hope you will enjoy exploring the Indian Ocean with us.

Gerald R. Allen
and
Roger C. Steene
*Perth, Australia*

# Acknowledgments

Numerous people have generously assisted our photographic efforts on various field trips. The majority of photos that appear in this book were taken between February and May, 1979, during a trip around the Indian Ocean. The National Science Foundation of the U.S. provided partial financial support for the senior author's participation by means of a grant to Dr. John E. Randall for a study of the wrasse genus *Coris*. Logistic assistance was provided by the following people: Dr. Boonprakob and his staff at the Phuket Marine Biological Center, Thailand; Dr. George De Bruin, Director of Fisheries Research, Sri Lanka; Mr. Ken Bock of Nairobi, Kenya; Mr. Daniel Pelicier of Mauritius; Prof. Margaret M. Smith, Dr. Phillip C. Heemstra, and Mr. Robin Stobbs of the J.L.B. Smith Institute of Ichthyology, Grahamstown, South Africa; Mr. Malcolm Smale, Port Elizabeth, South Africa; Monty and Cathy McKewon of Durban, South Africa; and Drs. Paddy Berry and Rudy Van Der Elst of the Oceanographic Research Institute, Durban.

Our work on Western Australian reefs was greatly assisted by Dr. Barry Wilson, Mr. Barry Hutchins, Mr. Neil Sarti, Mr. Pat Baker, Mr. Clay Bryce, all of the Western Australian Museum, Perth, and by Mr. John Braun (Perth), Mr. Barry Russell (Sydney), Rudie and Alison Kuiter (Sydney), and Bill and Eve Curry (Dampier, Western Australia). The junior author's work on the northern Great Barrier Reef and New Britain was assisted by Mr. Brian Parkinson and Dan and Gail Reardon of Rabaul; Roy and Susan O'Connor, formerly of Cairns, Queensland; Dr. Walter A. Starck II and his wife Janice of Daintree, Queensland; Mr. Ian Croll of "Reef World," Cairns; Mr. Paul Watson of "Shark World," Townsville; Mr. Dennis Wallace of Cairns; Richard and Rothe Schubot from Florida, U.S.A.; and Brian Lassig.

Several of the photos used in this book were taken by the junior author on a trip to the Philippines and Japan. Mr. Tim Hymes, Mr. Carl Ferraris, and Mr. Ed Murdy assisted in the Philippines, and the Japanese work was aided by Mr. Jack Moyer and Miss Martha Zaiser.

The senior author traveled to the Red Sea and Persian Gulf in 1975 and 1977. Mr. David Fridman of Coral World, Elat, Israel, provided valuable diving assistance on the first trip. The latter visit was financed by the FAO of the United Nations under the supervision of Dr. Walter Fischer. Assistance on this trip was given by Dr. John Randall, Dr. William Smith-Vaniz, and by Dr. Peter Vine and his wife Paula.

We are also grateful to the Australian National Parks and Wildlife Service for providing financial and logistic assistance that enabled us to visit Christmas Island. Special thanks are due Mr. Vance Russell of the Parks Service and Mr. Frank Boyle, the island's Government Administrator, for their organizational efforts. We especially appreciate the helpfulness and generosity of various island residents including Mr. Dave Allison, Mr. Geoff Deal, Mr. Mike Kitney, and Mr. Keith Moller.

Dr. John Randall of the Bishop Museum, Honolulu, and Drs. Douglass Hoese and Jeff Leis of the Australian Museum, Sydney, helped us to identify photographs of parrotfishes, gobies, and porcupinefishes respectively. Mr. Martin Thompson of Perth prepared the excellent color paintings of sharks, rays, and game fishes, and also the map of the Indian Ocean. Miss Roxanne Bibbey compiled the index. Lastly, we thank Mrs. Connie Allen who prepared the typescript and assisted with proofreading.

10

**Chapter One**

# *The Environment*

**Introduction**

The Indian Ocean is the smallest of the world's three major oceans, but its physical statistics are impressive nevertheless. Covering 75 million square kilometers (29 million square miles), its vast width stretches some 8,000 km (5,000 miles) from the shores of Western Australia to the East African coast. Although modern jet travel has greatly shortened the distance around this great basin, the Indian Ocean in many respects remains an area of mystery and intrigue far removed from the beaten path. This is not to say the region is totally unknown. Indeed, a growing number of travelers, particularly from western European countries, are sampling its unique beauty and diverse cultures. Fortunately the region has largely avoided the fanfare of tour promotions and gross commercialism now running rampant at many tropical Pacific and Caribbean localities. Although not well publicized at this stage, there are ample accommodations available and facilities for diving at most of the principal island groups. From the jungle-clad mountains and surrounding aquamarine coral reefs of the Comores to the lonely desert islands along the West Australian coast, this huge region offers the diving traveler countless opportunities for adventure and discovery.

At the onset of this project we endeavored to gather as much information as possible about the major island areas of the Indian Ocean, particularly with reference to the best diving. Aside from encyclopedic-type facts gleaned from travel agents and reference books, we found little information of practical value. We did receive a few helpful hints from fellow divers who had recently visited some of the islands, but apart from that it was largely guesswork. Where should we go? This was a question we answered on the basis of several criteria: (1) are there any coral reefs and is the water likely to be clear? (2) are SCUBA tanks and compressors available? and, most important, (3) is the location within reach of regular commercial air services? It was our intention to make a wide sampling of localities across the breadth of the Indian Ocean. We ultimately selected Phuket Island (Thailand), Sri Lanka, the Maldive Islands, the Seychelles, Mauritius, Kenya, and South Africa. We wanted to visit Madagascar as well, but eventually scuttled these plans because of political unrest on the island. Our coverage of the poorly known eastern Indian Ocean was given a tremendous boost in the form of a grant from the Australian National Parks and Wildlife Service that enabled us to visit Christmas Island. Also, we were able to include limited coverage of the waters surrounding the Arabian Peninsula thanks to the Food and Agricultural Organization of the United Nations, which invited one of us (GRA) to participate in a fisheries survey of that area.

**The Islands and Their People**

Compared with the tropical western Pacific, which literally teems with thousands of islands, there are relatively few islands in the Indian Ocean. Still, they number approximately 3,000, of which about 2,000 make up the coral reef atolls of the Maldives. The major islands and island groups include the Comores, Madagascar, Mauritius-Reunion, Seychelles, Laccadives, Maldives, Chagos, Sri Lanka, Andamans, Nicobars, and the Cocos-Keeling and Christmas Islands. These areas can be conveniently divided into two major groups on the basis of their topography: (1) mountainous or hilly islands and (2) low-lying coral islands. All of the areas listed above fall into the first category except the Maldive-Laccadive-Chagos chain and the Cocos-Keeling Group. The high islands are carpeted with lush tropical greenery and provide scenic coastal vistas with mountain peaks often rising sharply from the edge of the sea. They are either volcanic in origin, for example Mauritius and Reunion, or represent a cut-off portion of a major continental block, as is the case of Madagascar and the Comores. Perhaps the most interesting islands, at least from a marine scientist's point of view, are the low-lying atolls constructed through eons of time by a myriad of small animals—the reef-building corals. Atolls originate as fringing coral reefs that surround volcanic islands. Over a vast period these island ramparts and the surrounding reef gradually subside into the depths. However, because the rate of sinking is infinitesimally slow and that of coral growth relatively rapid, the fringing band of reef is able to literally keep its head above water. Successive generations of coral are eroded and compacted, thus providing a foundation for further reef construction in spite of the gradual submergence and eventual disappearance of the central volcanic core. The end result is a ring of coral reefs at or just below the surface of the sea. The volcanic origin of atoll formation has been confirmed by drilling operations. At Enewetak Atoll in the Pacific the drill finally contacted volcanic rock after it had passed through 1,080 meters of coral limestone. During storms limestone boulders and coral heads are tossed onto shallow reefs, thus facilitating the deposit of sand and debris on which terrestrial organisms can gain a foothold. Most atoll islands range in elevation only from about 1 to 5 meters. The typical vegetation consists of low scrub growth and coconut palms.

Equally as diverse as the landscape are the 22 million human inhabitants of the Indian Ocean. This impressive figure is somewhat deceptive as the large majority of people are congregated on the two largest islands: nearly seven million on Madagascar and 13 million on Sri Lanka. As a result most of the other islands are sparsely inhabited. For example,

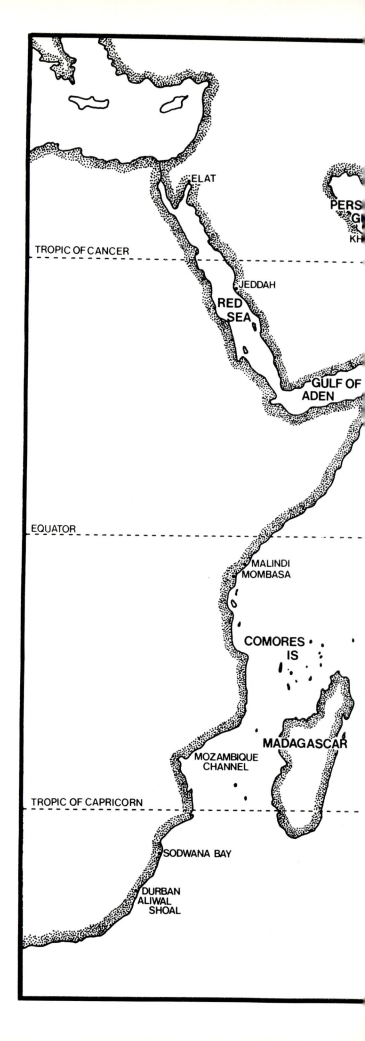

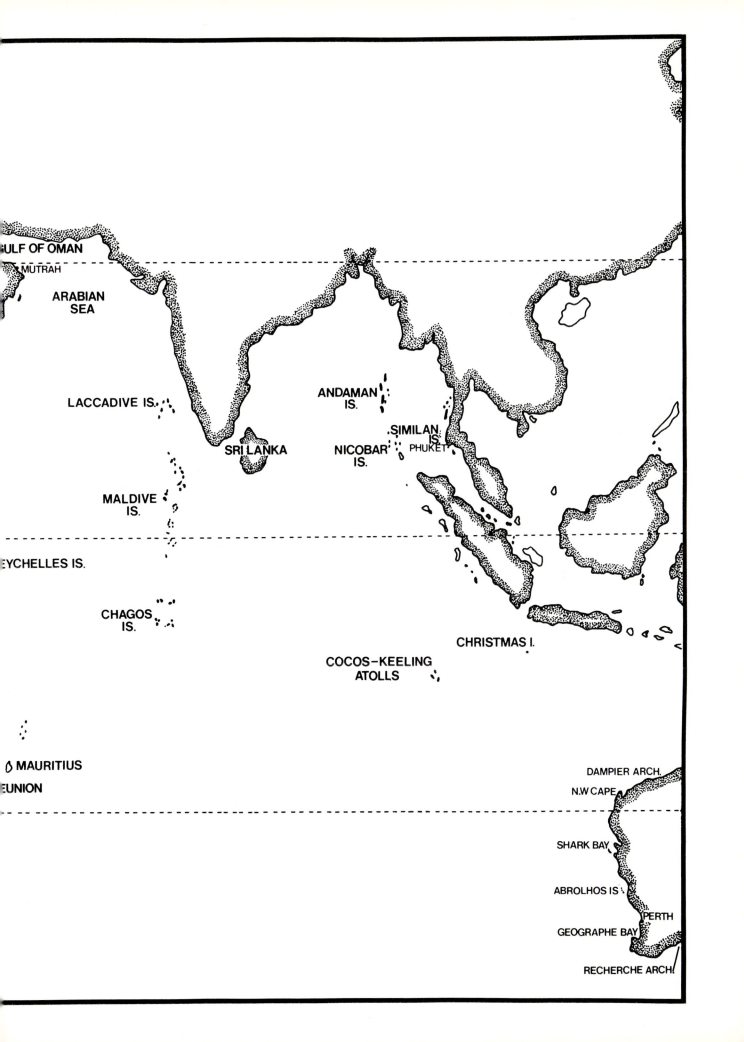

GULF OF OMAN

MUTRAH

ARABIAN
SEA

LACCADIVE IS.

ANDAMAN
IS.

SIMILAN
IS.

SRI LANKA

NICOBAR
IS.

PHUKET

MALDIVE
IS.

SEYCHELLES IS.

CHAGOS
IS.

CHRISTMAS I.

COCOS-KEELING
ATOLLS

MAURITIUS

REUNION

DAMPIER ARCH.

N.W CAPE

SHARK BAY

ABROLHOS IS

PERTH

GEOGRAPHE BAY

RECHERCHE ARCH.

the 210 inhabited atolls of the Maldives boast a population of only 106,000. Many of the smaller islands are uninhabited. We had the good fortune of spending several days at the Similans, a chain of hilly jungle-covered islets offshore from the Thailand-Burma border. It was hard to believe that such fertile islands with their surrounding crystalline waters and rich coral reefs remained unsettled. The variety of peoples and their cultures around the Indian Ocean seems nearly endless, ranging from the Negrito inhabitants of the Andamans and Nicobars, who are primitive forest hunters, to the sophisticated Europeans who have settled throughout the region. Many of the islands present a colorful cosmopolitan blend. For example, Mauritius and the Seychelles are populated by Indians, Europeans, Chinese, and an interesting Creole mixture. In spite of their proximity to Africa, the native inhabitants of Madagascar are of Malayo-Polynesian stock, more closely resembling Indonesians than their neighbors across the 400-kilometer-wide Mozambique Channel. The people of the Maldives, Laccadives, and Sri Lanka have Indian or Singhalese features. Those living in the Andaman Sea have Asian or Malayan characteristics. Tiny Christmas Island and the Cocos-Keeling Group were uninhabited until the last century but are now settled primarily by Malayans and a small number of Europeans. The major island areas are now mainly independent nations, although the Laccadives and Andaman-Nicobars remain under Indian jurisdiction and the Christmas-Cocos Islands are territories of Australia. Nevertheless, the colonial era has left an indelible influence on the entire area. British and French customs, language, and place names remain an integral part of island life in such places as Madagascar, Mauritius, Reunion, and the Seychelles.

This book is concerned mainly with the insular areas of the Indian Ocean, but the surrounding continental shores are deserving of at least brief mention. To round out our photographic coverage we visited a number of random localities on the margin of this vast region—the southwestern coast of Australia; Thailand in Southeastern Asia; the Persian Gulf, Arabian Sea, and Red Sea in the Middle East; and Kenya and Natal on the east Afri-

can coast. The surrounding rim of this great ocean offers a kaleidoscope of changing scenery and cultures. The West Australian coast is characterized by long sandy stretches punctuated with rocky headlands and mangrove inlets. Along much of the Asian coast there are jungle-covered peaks sloping gradually to the edge of the sea and endless miles of mangrove swamp. The Arabian coast is perhaps the starkest in all the world, but in many ways is among the most beautiful. Rugged, barren peaks rise steeply from the coast along much of the Red and Arabian Seas. In other parts of this region sandy desert or low flat scrub dunes are typical. The extensive African coastline includes a blend of all the previously mentioned landscapes. There are vast desert areas in the north, mangroves along much of the central portion, and near the southern tip the scenery is reminiscent of some of the Australian coast.

**Fish Habits and Habitats**

During 1978 we conducted a faunal survey of tiny Christmas Island, which lies in the northeastern corner of the Indian Ocean some 290 km south of the Indonesian island of Java. Although the fauna there is limited in terms of species numbers, mainly because of the small size of the island, it is in many respects typical of other tropical Indo-Pacific reefs. Therefore, it is instructive to summarize our results.

The great majority of Christmas Island fishes and those found on other Indian Ocean reefs are diurnal species that either dwell on the surface of the coral reef or forage on plankton a short distance above it. This category commonly includes such groups as the damselfishes, butterflyfishes, angelfishes, blennies, surgeonfishes, triggerfishes, filefishes, puffers, snappers, hawkfishes, triplefins, and most of the wrasses, groupers, and gobies. Approximately 62% of the fishes recorded at Christmas Island were in this category. Another 20% is composed of cryptic and nocturnal species that during daylight periods are confined primarily to caverns and reef crevices. Many of these are never seen by divers unless they are flushed from their lairs with chemical ichthyocides such as those frequently utilized by scientists. This assemblage includes such families as the cusk eels, some groupers and their relatives (*e.g.*, Plesiopidae, Pseudochromidae, Pseudogrammidae, etc.), most of the moray eels, and some scorpionfishes, wrasses (*Wetmorella*), and nocturnal families including the squirrelfishes, cardinalfishes, and sweeps (Pempheridae). Another important category contains species that dwell primarily on reefs covered with sand or rubble. Habitat diversity is comparatively low in these areas and they consequently tend to support a relatively low number of species. Nevertheless, approximately 10% of the Christmas Island species, including the snake eels, worm eels, various rays, lizardfishes, grubfishes (Parapercidae), flatfishes, and some wrasses and gobies, belongs to this category. A relatively small percentage (about 5%) of the fauna is composed of transient mid-water reef species that roam over large areas. This group includes most sharks, jacks, fusiliers, barracudas, and a scattering of representatives of other families.

During the past 10 years the senior author has been involved with ecological and taxonomic studies of damselfishes. This diverse group is extremely abundant on tropical reefs and exhibits certain ecological traits that are common to all reef fishes. The occurance of a given species is largely influenced by habitat factors that include salinity, type of substrate, and depth. Mangrove swamps, coastal embayments, and harbors frequently have fluctuating salinities influenced by local stream runoff. Although these areas support a substantial fish fauna, the composition is not nearly as diverse as that of coral reefs. It is the permanent habitat for many species of mullets, ponyfishes (Leiognathidae), mojarras (Gerriidae), whitings, and herrings, but also offers temporary refuge for legions of juvenile fishes that utilize this habitat as a nursery ground and later migrate to reef areas. The mangrove jack (*Lutjanus argentimaculatus*) is a typical member of the latter category.

Although some reef species occur over a wide variety of bottom types, many exhibit a highly specialized substrate preference. Major bottom habitats include sand or silt, coral rubble, limestone reef flats with varying degrees of porosity, weed beds, dead coral formations, and well developed areas of soft and hard corals. Frequently there is a complex mixture of two or more of these habitat types. The depth factor is also important. Many reef fishes exhibit relatively narrow depth range preferences. For example, in the damselfish family a relatively small percentage of species is mainly confined to shallow reef flat and tide pool areas that are under the influence of the breaking surf. Another small group of species prefers the deep outer reef slopes of oceanic islands and atolls and seldom ventures above 20 or 30 meters depth. Others are confined to shallow sandy lagoons with occasional coral patches. The great majority of damselfishes and reef fishes in general occur in areas of rich coral growth at depths between about three and 15 meters. In summary, the number of species encountered on a given section of reef is extremely variable and directly reflects habitat diversity and the availability of food.

# Chapter Two

# *Sharks and Rays*

Sharks and rays are among the most primitive fishes inhabiting global seas. Unlike the great majority of modern fishes that possess a bony skeleton, they are supported by a framework of cartilage that sometimes becomes secondarily calcified. Occasional shark attacks, a host of books and articles devoted to this subject, and the film production *Jaws* have focused much attention on sharks in the past few years. In spite of this fanfare there are relatively few dangerous sharks. Although the threat of shark attack is certainly a real one, it is frequently overexaggerated. It often seems as though the news media strive to convey the impression that tropical seas literally teem with man-eating sharks constantly in search of a meal. Of the approximately 350 species of sharks, only a few, mainly belonging to the families Carcharhinidae and Lamnidae, are considered dangerous. Even with the dangerous species, attacks are rare and generally occur under unusual circumstances, for example in traumatic situations where human blood is released into the water or if lured by the spearfishing activity of divers. The huge majority of shark encounters consist of brief confrontations without attack or injury and go unreported. Nevertheless, there are a few species that have been implicated in a number of attacks over the years and should be given a wide berth. These include the Great White Shark, Mako, and Tiger Shark .

The Indian Ocean is inhabited by numerous species of both sharks and rays. There are perhaps as many as 130 sharks and approximately half as many rays known in this region. Many species are seldom seen due to their deep-dwelling or pelagic mode of life. In the following section and in the illustrations that accompany this chapter relatively few species are represented. Most of these are common inhabitants of Indian Ocean reefs, except the Whale and Oceanic White-tip sharks, which are basically pelagic animals.

## SHARKS

**Whale Shark (*Rhiniodon typus;* family Rhiniodontidae)**—the largest modern fish known to man. Reaches a maximum size of at least 14 meters, but most sightings are of 5-10 meter individuals. It is a filter feeder on crustaceans and small fishes. Not dangerous to man.

**Great White Shark (*Carcharodon carcharias;* family Lamnidae)**—the largest of the dangerous sharks. Reaches a maximum size of about seven meters. Feeds mainly on fishes, particularly other sharks. This is the species that served as the model for *Jaws.*

**Mako Shark (*Isurus oxyrinchus;* family Lamnidae)**—another large, dangerous shark found both inshore and well out to sea. Has a pointed snout and dagger-like teeth used for catching fish prey. Grows to about 3-4 meters.

**Tiger Shark (*Galeocerdo cuvieri;* family Carcharhinidae)**—this dangerous shark has bars or spots on its sides. A notorious scavenger that feeds on a wide assortment of items. Bottles and tin cans are often found among the stomach contents. Grows to about 5.5 meters.

**Oceanic White-tip Shark (*Carcharhinus longimanus;* family Carcharhinidae)**—easily recognized by the fin markings and huge pectoral fins. A pelagic species often found in the open ocean far from land. Grows to about 3.5 meters and is considered dangerous.

**Black-tip Shark (*Carcharhinus melanopterus;* family Carcharhinidae)**—perhaps the most common shallow water shark on reef flats of the tropical Indo-Pacific. Grows to about two meters and not usually considered dangerous, but on occasion will attack splashing waders.

**Grey Reef Shark (*Carcharhinus amblyrhynchos:* family Carcharhinidae)**—a common inhabitant of the outer or seaward reef slope. Can be dangerous if provoked or if attracted by spearfishing. Grows to about 2.5 meters.

**Silver-tip Shark (*Carcharhinus albimarginatus;* family Carcharhinidae)**—usually found in habitats similar to the previous species, but in slightly deeper water. A very curious shark that is easily provoked. Grows to about three meters.

**Reef White-tip Shark (*Triaenodon obesus;* family Carcharhinidae)**—a common inhabitant of shallow reefs. Sometimes seen resting motionless on the bottom in caves. Grows to about 2.5 meters and is not considered dangerous.

**Lemon Shark (*Negaprion acutidens;* family Carcharhinidae)**—common on shallow coral reefs. Quickly recognized by the nearly equal size of the two dorsal fins. Grows to about three meters and is usually not a threat to man although attacks in the Atlantic have been reported.

**Zebra Shark (*Stegostoma varium;* family Orectolobidae)**—the brightly patterned juveniles are responsible for the common name. Sometimes seen lying motionless on sandy bottoms. Feeds mainly on molluscs and not dangerous to man. Grows to nearly three meters.

**Hammerhead Shark (*Sphyrna* spp.; family Sphyrnidae)**—two common species on Indian Ocean reefs, the Smooth Hammerhead (*S. zygaena*) and Scalloped Hammerhead (*S. lewini*). Both are considered dangerous and grow to about 3-4 meters.

## RAYS

**Manta Ray (*Manta alfredi;* family Mobulidae)**—may attain an enormous size of over 3,000 pounds with a "wingspan" in excess of 6.5 meters. An inhabitant of the open sea, but frequently seen near reefs. Frequently leaps entirely out of the water. Feeds on plankton.

**Cow-nose Ray (*Rhinoptera neglecta;* family Myliobatidae)**—a moderately large ray with a protruding double-lobed head. Feeds on clams, crabs, lobsters, oysters, and other benthic-dwelling invertebrates. Attains a "wingspan" of about two meters.

**Spotted Eagle Ray (*Stoasodon narinari;* family Myliobatidae)**—a beautiful free-swimming ray often seen cruising in the vicinity of coral reefs. The diet is similar to that of the preceding species. The maximum "wingspan" is about 3.5 meters.

**Coach-whip Ray (*Himantura uarnak;* family Dasyatidae)**—a bottom-dweller of sandy flats. Attains a disc width of about 1.5-2.0 meters. The long tail is equipped with a poisonous barb near its base.

**Blue-spot Ray (*Taeniura lymma;* family Dasyatidae)**—a common inhabitant of shallow coral reefs. Often seen lying motionless on the bottom under coral heads. Attains a length of about 2.5 meters.

**Black-spot Ray (*Taeniura melanospila;* family Dasyatidae)**—a sand-dwelling ray with an oval-shaped disc covered with dark mottling. Attains a disc width of 1.5-2.0 meters.

**Electric Ray (*Torpedo marmoratus;* family Torpedinidae)**—usually dwells on mud flats or sandy areas. Is capable of producing a powerful electric shock and therefore should not be handled. Grows to a length of about 0.7 meters.

**Guitarfish (*Rhyncobatus djeddensis;* family Rhinobatidae)**—an unusual shaped ray sometimes seen lying on sandy bottoms in the vicinity of coral reefs. The diet consists mainly of molluscs. Grows to three meters in length.

# Chapter Three

# *Game Fishes*

Our species coverage encompasses mainly coral reef dwellers, but there remains one important segment of the Indian Ocean fauna that should not be neglected—the game fishes. This term is used for a diverse assemblage of species that provide sport or recreation and also forms the basis of valuable commercial fisheries. There are many different species from a wide range of families included in this category with a high percentage of the game fishes found in the jack family (Carangidae), tuna family (Scombridae), billfish families (Xiphiidae and Istiophoridae), and the dolphinfish family (Coryphaenidae). Without exception these are sleek, powerful pelagic species capable of fast swimming speeds. Most are excellent table fishes with firm white or pink flesh. Another feature common to many of these fishes is the presence of countershading, a combination of darkish coloration, usually black or blue, on the top part of the body, and whitish or silvery hues on the ventral portion. Countershading serves to camouflage these fishes in the open-sea environment. They blend in with the deep blue of the ocean depths when viewed from above and the silvery mirror-like reflections of the surface when viewed from below. This pattern no doubt is advantageous in hunting down small prey fishes and also for avoiding detection from large predators such as sharks.

## Jacks (family Carangidae)

The jacks or trevallies are a large family represented in all tropical and temperate seas. Most of the popular angling species belong to the genera *Carangoides* and *Caranx* (true Jacks), *Elagatis* (Rainbow Runner), *Scomberoides* (Queenfishes and Leatherskins), *Trachinotus* (Darts and Pompanos), and *Seriola* (Kingfishes and Amberjacks). These groups generally include the larger members of the family. The Noble Trevally (*Caranx ignobilis*) is one of the largest, reaching a length of nearly two meters. The family also contains a number of smaller species, for example members of the genera *Decapterus*, *Selar*, and *Selaroides*, that grow to 20-30 cm and are sometimes referred to as scads. A few carangid species are found in the open sea many miles from land, but the majority occur in the vicinity of reefs, often cruising the perimeter in large schools. They feed primarily on small fishes, but at least one species, the Toothless Golden Trevally (*Gnathanodon speciosus*), feeds largely on benthic crustaceans.

## Tunas and Mackerels (family Scombridae)

Most of the true tunas and mackerels are inhabitants of the high seas. Their powerfully muscled, streamlined bodies are capable of speeds approaching 48 km per hour. Species such as the Frigate Mackerel (*Auxis thazard*), Little Tuna (*Euthynnus affinis*), Skipjack Tuna (*Katsuwonis pelamis*), Albacore (*Thunnus alalunga*), Yellowfin Tuna (*T. albacares*), Bluefin Tuna (*T. maccoyii*), Bigeye Tuna (*T. obesus*), and Longtail Tuna (*T. tonggol*) form a substantial portion of the commercial fishery in the Indo-Pacific region. A few species, such as the Dogtooth Tuna (*Gymnosarda unicolor*), Shark Mackerel (*Grammatorcynus bicarinatus*), Reef Mackerel (*Rastrelliger kanagurta*), Slimy Mackerel (*Scomber australasicus*), and the several species of Spanish Mackerel (*Scomberomorus*), are commonly found on the edge of the reef or inshore. They provide good sport for recreational anglers and spearfishermen. The Spanish Mackerels are seasonably abundant in some localities such as the Persian Gulf and are often taken in large quantities by commercial fishermen.

## Billfishes (families Xiphiidae and Istiophoridae)

This group includes the largest and most highly prized game fishes. The Swordfish is the sole member of the family Xiphiidae. It inhabits cool temperate and subtropical waters of all seas. The maximum size is about five meters. They have been known to attack small boats with their elongate, spear-like snout. The marlins and sailfishes belong to the family Istiophoridae. They migrate over vast distances and are locally common only at certain times of the year. For example, the waters outside the Great Barrier Reef off Cairns, Queensland, provide some of the best marlin fishing found anywhere in the world. However, due to the migratory patterns of these fishes the season is limited to only three months (approximately September to November). The Black and Blue Marlins are the kings of this family in terms of weight, the largest specimens approaching a ton! These fishes feed primarily on various fishes (juvenile tuna are a favorite item), squid, and crustaceans.

## Dolphinfish (family Coryphaenidae)

The two species of dolphinfish are inhabitants of the high seas in tropical latitudes. They are excellent fighting fishes and for this reason are much sought after by anglers. Dolphinfish are sometimes found in the vicinity of logs, seaweed "rafts," and other floating debris. They are attracted by small fishes that swarm around these objects. Maximum size is about two meters. Males have more vivid colors and a blunter, steeper head profile than females.

# Chapter Four

# *Eels*

Most people associate the word "eel" with a group of fishes popularly referred to as the morays. They are well known because of their conspicuous habits, large size, and reputation of being dangerous to man. However, the morays are just one of more than 20 eel families inhabiting the world's seas. All share certain anatomical peculiarities which include an elongate snake-like body, usually a lack of scales, an absence of pelvic fins, and the anal and dorsal fins usually continuous with the tail fin (if present). In addition, most eels have a strange flattened, transparent larval stage known as a leptocephalus.

Four major eel groups are common on tropical Indian Ocean reefs. Of these only the morays and to a lesser extent the snake eels are truly conspicuous. The moray eels (family Muraenidae) are represented by approximately 50-60 species in the tropical Indian Ocean. They are by far the largest eels, with some species, such as *Gymnothorax javanicus* and *G. tessellata*, attaining a weight of 23 kg and a length of over 2 m, with rare reports of individuals up to 3 m. Morays have the largely undeserved reputation of being aggressive toward humans and are sometimes classed with sharks and barracudas as being the most vicious fishes in the sea. It is true that many species possess tremendously powerful jaws equipped with needle-like teeth, but these are adaptations normally used for capturing small fishes or invertebrates that are swallowed whole. Morays are usually passive creatures that if left unprovoked pose no threat to a diver's safety. The relatively few attacks that have occurred are usually the result of mistaken identity when the victim suddenly dangles a hand in front of or down into the moray's lair, or when the eel is obviously provoked, for example when speared or prodded. Of course nature always has its exceptions, and from our experience there is one moray species that could be classed as aggressive. *Gymnothorax breedeni* frequently exhibits a nasty disposition and will sometimes go out of its way to harass a diver who decides to spend more than a few moments in its territory. We both received minor bites on the hands and legs by this eel at Christmas Island and the Maldives while kneeling on the bottom during photographic sessions.

Other eel residents of the tropical Indian Ocean are less conspicuous. The burrowing snake eels (family Ophichthidae) are represented by about 40-50 species and generally dwell in sandy areas at the reef edge. Some are brightly banded or spotted, but the majority are rather drab, unspectacular creatures. Many species bear a strong spike-like tail that is used to burrow backward through the sand. Their maximum length is usually less than one meter. They subsist largely on a diet of small crustaceans and fishes that are often captured at night.

The worm eels (family Moringuidae) are similar in habit to the snake eels but generally are much more slender in shape and smaller. Some species are pink, and they possess very small eyes. The overall impression is that of a large earthworm. There are fewer than 10 species in the tropical Indian Ocean.

The only other eel group deserving mention is the congers (family Congridae). There are approximately 12 species in the tropical Indian Ocean, most of which are largely gray in color and inhabit reef crevices, much like the moray eels. Members of the specialized subfamily Heterocongrinae are known as garden eels and inhabit sandy burrows. They often occur in large colonies that feed on drifting plankton.

# Chapter Five

# *Squirrelfishes*

Squirrelfishes are present in all tropical seas, with most species occurring in the Indo-Pacific region. They are small to medium-sized fishes generally characterized by bright red colors and large eyes. The dorsal fin includes a spiny anterior portion that is often folded down and separated from the soft posterior rays by a deep notch. These fishes are basically nocturnal, sheltering in caves, under ledges, or under tabular *Acropora* coral during daylight hours. At dusk they begin patrolling the open reef in search of prey, which consists mainly of crabs, shrimps, gastropods, polychaetes, and occasional small fishes. They generally hunt alone or in small groups but during the day may form large aggregations in dark caverns. If these groups are disturbed by a diver they emit a clearly audible staccato noise. This chattering type sound in combination with the large eyes is the basis of the name "squirrelfish," although in some areas they are also known as soldierfishes. Little is known about their reproductive habits, but both eggs and larvae are known to be pelagic. The advanced larval stages are easily captured by attracting them to a light suspended just below the surface at night. The 2-cm-long larvae are silvery in color with a peculiar elongate beak. These young squirrelfishes are often eaten by tunas.

About 30 species belonging to five genera are known to occur in the Indian Ocean. *Sargocentron* ( = *Adioryx*) and *Myripristis* are by far the largest genera, each with about one dozen species. These fishes, particularly *Myripristis*, although not particularly large (to about 45 cm, usually under 30 cm), are considered good eating and are commonly offered for sale in fish markets. They are usually caught with either hook and line or traps. The genus *Neoniphon* contains three species, of which *N. sammara* is the most common in the Indian Ocean. The remaining genera are *Plectrypops*, *Corniger* (Atlantic genus), *Pristilepis*, and *Ostichthys*.

# Chapter Six

# *Pipefishes, Seahorses, and Allies*

The family Syngnathidae, popularly known as pipefishes and seahorses, contains approximately 90 species in the Indian Ocean, making it one of the largest groups found there. In spite of the large number of species they are inconspicuous members of the reef community because of their small size (usually under 20 cm) and secretive habits. Pipefishes are long and slender with a bony exterior divided into numerous segments. The snout is characteristically tube-like and in many species is rather elongate. Seahorses are structurally very similar to pipefishes but have the head enlarged and positioned at an angle. Typically, syngnathids have a low, inconspicuous dorsal fin composed only of soft rays and a pair of pectoral fins just behind the head. Some species possess a caudal fin and a rudimentary anal fin. Sometimes the pectorals, anal, or caudal fin is absent, and a small number of species lack fins entirely. The members of the family are found in a wide variety of habitats including brackish estuaries, weed flats, and coral and rocky reefs, and several are regularly encountered in freshwater streams. The reproductive habits of these fishes are well known. The female generally deposits a small number of eggs in a specialized brood pouch on the ventral surface of the male. Some species lack a pouch and the eggs are carried in an exposed position. The eggs are thus incubated by the male parent until hatching, which requires several weeks. Most pipefishes and seahorses feed on tiny planktonic crustaceans such as copepods, isopods, and ostracods.

There are at least 35 genera of pipefishes and seahorses inhabiting the Indian Ocean. Most contain only one to four species. The largest groups are the seahorse genus *Hippocampus* (about 12 species) and the pipefish genera *Syngnathus* (10-15 species) and *Corythoichthys* (six species). The latter group contains the most conspicuous pipefishes on shallow coral reefs; these are often seen swimming slowly across the bottom in serpent-like fashion. Because of their reduced finnage they are poor swimmers and it is possible to capture specimens barehanded. The bizarre Leafy Sea Dragon (*Phycodurus eques*) of Southern Australia is by far the most spectacular member of the family. Its leafy appendages greatly resemble the kelp among which it lives. Nearly as strange in appearance are the ghost pipefishes belonging to the family Solenostomidae. At lest two species are known from shallow waters of the eastern Indian Ocean.

# Chapter Seven

# *Scorpionfishes*

Scorpionfishes are perhaps best known for the venomous properties of the fin spines found in many species. The most notorious in this respect are the stonefishes belonging to the subfamily Synanceiinae. Although few people have been unlucky enough to tread on the spines, there are several published reports of stings accompanied by excruciating pain and convulsive death within several minutes. The active ingredient of the poison is a protein which is broken down and rendered inactive by heating. Therefore the recommended treatment for scorpionfish stings is immediate immersion in very hot (not scalding) water. Lionfishes belonging to the genera *Pterois* and *Dendrochirus*, although not as venomous as the stonefishes, are capable of dangerous stings which have rendered victims unconscious, resulting in severe swelling and a need for several days of hospitalization. These fishes are popular with aquarium hobbyists and therefore great caution should be exercised when handling them.

Most of the members of the family are small to medium in size, usually under about 30 cm. They are characterized by bony struts on the cheek bones and often there are small spinelets or filamentous skin appendages on the head. The anterior portion of the dorsal fin is composed of stout, spike-like spines and there is often a notch between the spinous and soft portions of the fin. The anal fin is preceded by three sharp spines, which also may be venomous. The pectoral fins are frequently thick and well developed. They may be used as a supporting structure while perching on the bottom or for cornering prey. Most scorpionfishes are red, brown, or gray in color or are patterned with a mottled combination of these colors. Many of the species exhibit elaborate camouflage coloration. Scorpionfishes are basically bottom dwellers, and all but a few lack a gas bladder. Most species are passive predators of crabs, shrimps, and small fishes. One species, *Iracundus signifer*, has evolved an incredible decoy mechanism that it uses to lure unsuspecting prey (see section on camouflage and mimicry). Lionfishes, or turkeyfishes as they are sometimes called, are primarily nocturnal feeders that roam over large areas of the bottom in search of crabs and small fishes. When thrust far forward their elaborate, oversized pectoral fins no doubt confuse their quarry and are effective in cutting off possible escape routes.

The family is one of the largest in the Indian Ocean with approximately 40 genera and 90-100 species. The largest groups are *Scorpaenodes* (about 12-15 species), *Scorpaena* (about 10 species), *Minous* (six species), and *Pterois* (five species). There are a number of allied families such as the velvetfishes (Aploactidae) and the Australian pigfishes (Congiopodidae) that greatly resemble the scorpaenids in overall appearance. Other common relatives of the scorpionfishes are the diminutive coral velvetfishes of the family Caracanthidae. These tiny inhabitants of coral reefs live among the branches of certain corals.

# Chapter Eight

# *Color Variation*

Both aquarists and scientists are often puzzled by the very different color patterns that may occur in a single species of reef fish. In many instances this sort of variation has been responsible for the application of two or more scientific or common names to the same species, thus causing a great deal of confusion in subsequent literature. Variation in color pattern is actually commonplace in tropical reef fishes and is associated with a number of factors that are discussed in the following paragraphs.

## Variation Related to Geography

Certain species, particularly those which are distributed over a wide area, are frequently characterized by different color patterns at widely separated localities. In most cases this type of variation involves relatively subtle changes in the basic pattern, although very different colorations may be evident at the opposite extremes of the distributional range. Geographic variation generally reflects at least a partial degree of isolation and may be indicative of the first stages of speciation. Given sufficient time (thousands of years) these population variants may evolve into separate species.

## Variation Related to Growth Stages

These are changes in color pattern that accompany the development from the juvenile to the adult stage. Many species of damselfishes and butterflyfishes possess a pale-rimmed dark ocellus on the dorsal fin as juveniles. This marking may persist into adulthood in a few species, but more often it gradually disappears with increased growth. This false "eyespot" may afford some degree of protection against predation for the young by

causing attacking fishes to focus their aggression at an area of low vulnerability (dorsal fin as opposed to the head). Perhaps the most striking juvenile–adult transformations are found in the angelfishes (family Pomacanthidae).

## Variation Related to Sex

Some species exhibit very different male-female color patterns. This phenomenon is most evident in fishes that are known to reverse sex during a certain stage of their life history. The most common type of reversal involves the transformation from a functional female to a more brightly colored functional male. This type of sex reversal is typical of fairy basslets (family Serranidae; subfamily Anthiinae), wrasses (Labridae), parrotfishes (Scaridae), and *Genicanthus* angelfishes (Pomacanthidae). Male to female changes have been documented in several species of anemonefishes (Pomacentridae), but there is little or no color difference between sexes.

## Variation Related to Ecological Conditions

Variation in pattern and the intensity of colors are influenced by a number of ecological factors including depth, type of substrate, turbidity, and time of day. Color intensity variation related to depth is common in many fishes, particularly among the groupers. Fishes dwelling in the sunlit shallows of the coral reef may be predominantly brown or gray whereas conspecifics from deeper areas of the reef often exhibit bright reds or pinks. This type of depth-related variation tends to be of a permanent nature. Changes related to substrate and turbidity, by contrast, are commonly short-lived. Some fishes show a very bleached out, drab coloration in low contrast situations (sand and rubble, for example) or in dirty water. Species such as flatfishes, anglerfishes, and flatheads are capable of rapid to gradual color changes that enable them to effectively blend in with the background, thus making it easier for them to capture the small fishes upon which they feed. Special night coloration is a characteristic of some reef fishes and is treated separately later.

## Variation Related to Behavior

The color pattern is sometimes temporarily altered according to behavioral mood. The best documented variation of this type is that found in male damselfishes (Pomacentridae) during courtship, spawning, and nest-guarding. Striking color shanges may occur during these activities, and the intensity of these changes is directly related to the intensity of the behavioral actions. The nuptial colors can be switched on and off instantaneously. The most intense color change is generally associated with nest- guarding activities. The capability of turning on bright spawning colors is found in the males of many reef fishes, particularly the fairy basslets, wrasses (especially *Cirrhilabrus)*, parrotfishes, and gobies.

## Chapter Nine

# *Groupers and Allies*

The serranid fishes or groupers represent one of the largest families of coral reef-dwellers. It is estimated that in the Indian Ocean alone there are 130-140 species belonging to slightly over 30 genera. They range in size from tiny *Luzonichthys*, which mature at under 5 cm, to the gargantuan *Promicrops*, weighing up to half a ton and attaining a length of over two meters. Most of the larger groupers are brown, black, or gray in color, often spotted or mottled. However, the fairy perchlets or basslets of the subfamily Anthiinae are among the most colorful of reef fishes, exhibiting an array of bright reds, pinks, and yellows. The groupers are considered to be very generalized bony fishes without the special modifications present in many of the more advanced teleosts. They are somewhat laterally compressed with moderately elongate bodies and are characterized, at least in the larger species, by a huge mouth. There is a single dorsal fin usually containing seven to 12 spines with a number of soft rays behind. The soft anal rays are preceded by three spines. Most groupers are benthic predators that lurk in caverns, under ledges, or among coral waiting for passing prey in the form of small fishes and invertebrates. An exception is the fairy basslets or anthiine fishes, which include about one dozen genera, the largest of which is *Anthias* with about 15 species in the Indian Ocean. Most of the members of this subfamily are relatively small, delicate, schooling fishes that swarm well above the bottom in search of planktonic food. If disturbed, for example by the presence of a diver, they quickly retreat to the shelter of the reef below.

The genus *Epinephelus* contains an estimated 45-50 Indian Ocean species, many of which are favorite food fishes. They are usually caught by hook and line or by underwater spearfishing. *Cephalopholis*, with about 12-15 species, and the three species of *Plectropoma* are also highly esteemed because of their excellent table qualities.

One of the remarkable characteristics of the serranids is their ability to reverse sex. Some species have both male and female reproductive organs and can function as either sex or even both sexes at the same time. Sex reversal is common among the anthiine fishes, which are characterized by different male and female color patterns. A single male is often surrounded by a harem of females that exhibit a "peck order" system of dominance. If the male is killed or experimentally removed, the top-ranking female changes color and becomes a functional male, a very convenient mode of species perpetuation. Courtship in these fishes is very colorful, with males engaging in dramatic displays in which the fins are fully erected.

The family Grammistidae contains five Indian Ocean genera each with a single species. Those illustrated here include *Belonoperca*, *Grammistes*, and *Pogonoperca*. They generally resemble small groupers and are commonly called "soapfishes" because of their slimy exterior mucous coat. The mucus is bitter tasting and has toxic properties, thus affording some measure of protection against predation. The Pseudochromidae ("dwarf groupers") is another serranid relative that inhabits Indian Ocean reefs. Approximately 40 species are known from the region. Most belong to the genera *Pseudochromis*, *Chlidichthys*, and *Labracinus*. All are small, secretive fishes that live under boulders and ledges or among dense coral. Many of the species exhibit brilliant colors and are favorites of aquarists. The members of the family Plesiopidae are similar in appearance to pseudochromids. There are less than one dozen species in the Indian Ocean and most are small, secretive cave-dwellers. The largest and one of the most spectacular species is the Blue Devil (*Paraplesiops meleagris*) of southern Australia, which grows to at least 35 cm. *Calloplesiops altivelis* is another attractive species well known to aquarists. It dwells on tropical reefs, and a recent study published by Dr. John McCosker of San Francisco's Steinhart Aquarium reveals that it effectively mimics the head of *Gymnothorax meleagris*, a species of moray eel.

The Kuhliidae and Teraponidae are serranoid families represented by a small number of species in the Indian Ocean. They are inhabitants of shallow rocky or sandy bottom shores, sometimes entering brackish estuaries or freshwater streams. The best known representatives of these groups are the Flagtail (*Kuhlia mugil*) and the Tigerfish (*Terapon jarbua*). The Glaucosomidae is the last family included in this chapter. Although they are not closely related to groupers, they resemble them somewhat in shape (particularly the head) and general habits. Only a few species are found in the Indian Ocean, all members of the genus *Glaucosoma*. The West Australian Jewfish (*G. hebraicum*) has a delicate flavor and rates as one of the top food fishes in the vicinity of Perth, Australia.

# Chapter Ten

# *Cardinalfishes and Bigeyes*

The family Apogonidae contains a diverse assemblage of fishes occurring in tropical and warm temperate seas. They are commonly known as cardinalfishes owing to the coloration of many of the species. Approximately 90 species belonging to 16 genera have been recorded from the Indian Ocean. Many of these have broad distributions that extend into the western Pacific. They range in size from only 3-4 cm to a maximum length of about 25 cm. All are voracious predators of small fishes and crustaceans, especially the smaller shrimps and crabs. The various species live in relatively narrow habitat zones related to depth and bottom composition. Some are restricted to tidepools and reef flats while others dwell at various levels on the deeper portions of the reef. Typically they are encountered during daylight hours in caverns, under ledges, among the spines of sea urchins, or among the branches of large coral heads. The species of *Rhabdamia* are small transparent fishes that form enormous aggregations and may swim up to several meters above the bottom. However, most other cardinalfishes are found solitarily or occur in pairs and small aggregations. They often remain motionless for extended periods while hovering a short distance above the bottom. Many species appear to be nocturnal, abandoning their daytime retreats at dusk to roam the reef in search of prey.

Cardinalfishes are among the few marine fish groups that demonstrate the unusual habit of oral egg incubation. An egg ball containing up to several hundred individual ova is deposited by the female and after fertilization is incubated for several days in the mouth cavity of the male. During this time, in which the male is unable to feed, the mouth is held slightly agape and the eggs are periodically juggled within the oral cavity. The young are presumably pelagic upon hatching, and the male is therefore relieved of further parental duties.

The Priacanthidae or bigeyes are nocturnal fishes that form small aggregations in caverns or hover near the reef surface during the day. At night they disperse in search of prey items that include octopus, shrimps, crabs, polychaete worms, and small fishes. The large eye and brilliant red coloration are adaptations to a nocturnal existence. Bigeyes are capable of a rapid color change that involves a general bleaching of the red to a drab pale gray. The family is represented by about 10 species and 3 genera in the Indian Ocean, but only two, *Priancanthus cruentatus* and *P. hamrur*, are common on coral reefs.

# Chapter Eleven

# *Mimicry and Camouflage*

The phenomenon of mimicry is one of the most fascinating subjects related to coral reef fishes. Although the concept has been familiar to terrestrial biologists for over a century, it has only been well documented in the sea during the past two decades. Essentially, mimicry involves two or more species, sometimes belonging to different genera or even families, that greatly resemble one another with regard to color pattern and shape. One of the species—known as the model—usually possesses a certain quality, such as a poisonous bite, venomous spines, or distasteful flesh, that guarantees a certain degree of immunity from predators. The mimic species is similarly avoided by predators because of its resemblance to the model even though it may be thoroughly palatable. Several common examples of mimicry found among Indian Ocean fishes are shown in the accompanying illustrations. One of the most remarkable cases involves the sharpnose pufferfish *Canthigaster valentini*, which, apparently because of its toxic flesh, is mimicked by the filefish *Paraluteres prionurus*. The two species are usually seen in close proximity and at first glance, at least, are exceedingly difficult to differentiate. Many of the reported cases involve a *Meiacanthus* blenny as the model that is mimicked by either other blennies, for example *Plagiotremus*, *Ecsenius*, or *Petroscirtes*, or by various reef species including juvenile coral breams (*Scolopsis*, Nemipteridae) and cardinalfishes (Apogonidae). *Meiacanthus* is equipped with a predator deterrent in the form of venom glands that are associated with its enlarged lower jaw canines.

Another example of mimicry involves juveniles of the surgeonfish *Acanthurus pyroferus* (Acanthuridae) and several species of *Centropyge* angelfishes (Pomacanthidae). It seems uncanny that the surgeonfish mimic has the ability to assume the very different color patterns of several angelfish species. The reason for this particular mimicry is not clear, but perhaps predators are partially discouraged by the angelfish's habit of staying close to cover and exposing itself only for brief periods.

A few predatory fishes utilize mimicry to gain access to unsuspecting victims. For example, the young of the snapper *Lutjanus bohar* mimic certain species of damselfishes of the genus *Chromis*. The latter are small schooling fishes that feed on zooplankton and are ignored by other small reef fishes. The snapper is able to seek out small prey fishes with consummate ease in its *Chromis* disguise. Mimicry of this type is known as aggressive mimicry. The parasite-picking cleaner wrasse *Labroides* is aggressively mimicked by the blenny *Aspidontus taeniatus*. The latter uses its disguise to approach fishes at close range and then suddenly darts forward to rip off a scale or piece of fin, items that form a substantial part of its diet.

A number of fishes have evolved color patterns and shapes that render them nearly invisible against the surrounding reef background. Several vivid examples of camouflage coloration are shown here. Particularly impressive are certain scorpionfishes (Scorpaenidae) that resemble weed-covered rocks. At least one species covers itself with a growth of real algae. Another, *Iracundus signifer*, combines its camouflage with an unusual dorsal fin shaped like a small fish. It serves as a decoy that lures unsuspecting prey fishes. The spectacular Leafy Sea Dragon of southern Australian seas is the undisputed king of camouflage. Its leafy appendages and bizarre shape are undetectable among natural kelp.

# Chapter Twelve

# *Snappers and Allies*

The snapper family Lutjanidae and its relatives are sometimes collectively referred to as lutjanoid fishes. This is a diverse assemblage that includes a number of genera and family groupings whose evolutionary relationships remain poorly understood. Thus, the classification that is discussed below can only be regarded as provisional. However, it reflects the concepts currently subscribed to by most investigators. Although they are of relatively little interest to marine aquarists, many of these fishes are noted for their savory taste and are therefore much sought-after by both commercial and amateur fishermen.

Fishes of the family Lutjanidae, commonly known as tropical snappers or simply snappers, occur throughout tropical seas and are well represented in the Indo-Pacific region. The Indian Ocean provides a home for approximately 42 species, of which about 25 belonging to the genus *Lutjanus* are abundant on coral reefs. The genera *Etelis* and *Pristipomoides* contain about eight Indian Ocean representatives that commonly inhabit deep trawling grounds and are often taken with the use of handlines. Because of the bright color of some of the species they are sometimes called "red snappers." They may grow to a length of nearly one meter and form an important part of the commercial catch in some areas. Several of the *Lutjanus* species, including *L. coccineus*, *L. erythropterus*, *L. malabaricus*, and *L. sebae*, are similar in color (primarily reddish or pink) and size and also inhabit deeper trawling grounds, although the young are sometimes present near shore. Most of the other *Lutjanus* species are associated with coral reefs and are abundant to depths of at least 30-40 meters. The distinctive characters of this genus include a single dorsal fin composed of 10 to 12 rigid spines and 11 to 16 soft rays, well developed canine teeth, prominent teeth on the vomer and palatines (i.e., roof of mouth), and (most species) a slight to distinct notch on the preopercle (cheek) margin. They are relatively colorful, and some species such as the brilliant yellow, blue-striped snapper *Lutjanus kasmira* form huge aggregations during daylight hours. At night these shoals break up and individual fish roam widely over the reef in search of prey, which consists primarily of various crustaceans and small fishes. The *Lutjanus* snappers readily take a fish-baited hook and are excellent food fishes. The colorful young of several species, including *L. bengalensis*, *L. gibbus*, *L. kasmira*, and *L. sebae*, make fine aquarium pets but soon outgrow their surroundings if properly fed. The mangrove habitat provides shelter for the young of *L. argentimaculatus*, *L. ehrenbergii*, and *L. fulvus*. With increasing growth the young fish move offshore to deeper reef areas. The juveniles of at least one species, *Lutjanus argentimaculatus*, popularly known as the Mangrove Jack, sometimes penetrates the lower reaches of freshwater streams and can therefore be successfully maintained in freshwater aquaria. On the island of Bahrain in the Persian Gulf the senior author encountered large (0.5-1.0 meter) adults of this species in a small freshwater pool about one kilometer from the sea. The genera *Aphareus*, *Macolor*, and *Symphorus* each contain a single species and are common snappers on coral reefs; they exhibit habits similar to the species of *Lutjanus*.

The fusiliers belonging to the family Caesionidae are close relatives of the lutjanids and, in fact, until just recently were included in this family by most taxonomists. They differ primarily in their more slender body shape, protractile mouth, and habit of forming large schools high above the bottom. The approximately 10 species occurring in the Indian Ocean are inhabitants of coral reefs and have their greatest abundance on the outer slopes, often adjacent to steep drop-offs. The diet is composed of various planktonic items gleaned from the passing currents. Most species belong to the genera *Caesio* and *Pterocaesio* and are usually under about 30 cm in length.

Another important but less colorful group of lutjanoid fishes is the porgies belonging to the family Sparidae. These are medium-sized fishes often silvery or pink in color with many species possessing molar-like teeth, at least on the posterior part of the jaws. Like other lutjanoids, many are esteemed as food fishes. Approximately 40 species inhabit the Indian Ocean, with the group having its greatest abundance off the East African coast. Our photographic coverage includes the genera *Chrysoblephus*, *Diplodus*, *Procostoma*, and *Rhabdosargus*.

The family Lethrinidae or emperors includes about 15-20 Indian Ocean representatives mostly belonging to the genus *Lethrinus*. These fishes are similar to the *Lutjanus* snappers in size, shape, and diet but generally lack bright colors, more often exhibiting various shades of gray. Although they are found in the vicinity of coral reefs, the preferred habitat consists of open sandy stretches between reefs. However, the Golden-line Emperor, *Gnathodentax aurolineatus*, and Big-eye Emperor, *Monotaxis grandoculis*, are usually encountered in the immediate vicinity of coral reefs. The members of the genus *Gymnocranius* are found both in sandy areas and on reefs. At some localities *Lethrinus* emperors are much sought after as table fish. The soft white flesh is of excellent quality. In Western Australia keen anglers frequently travel more than 1,000 miles from Perth to North West Cape for a few days of fishing for *Lethrinus nebulosus*, locally known as the "Norwest Snapper."

The family Nemipteridae is confined to the tropical Indo-West Pacific region and is well represented in the Indian Ocean, with at least 20 species occurring there. Most belong to the genus *Nemipterus*, a poorly studied group that is mainly associated with relatively deep, sandy trawling grounds sometimes situated well offshore and away from coral reefs. Of greater interest to reef enthusiasts are the coral breams belonging to the genera *Pentapodus* and *Scolopsis*. These fishes are solitary in habit, feeding mainly on small invertebrates such as crabs and shrimps and occasional small fishes. They move about the reef with characteristic quick darting movements interspersed with stops in which they hover for several seconds a short distance above the bottom. *Scolopsis bilineatus* is usually encountered on or close to the coral reef, whereas most of the other species prefer sandy areas between reefs. When feeding they often seize a mouthful of sand that is passed out via the gill openings.

The last group of lutjanoid fishes treated here are the sweetlips or grunters, which comprise the family Haemulidae, sometimes called the Plectorhynchidae. They are a worldwide circumtropical group with many representatives in both the Atlantic and Indo-Pacific. Most coral reef species in the latter region are included in the genus *Plectorhynchus*, which contains approximately 15 species, most of which occur in the tropical Indian Ocean. Some species may reach a maximum size of about one meter, and most are excellent eating fishes. Juveniles exhibit highly contrasted, bright color patterns and swim in undulating fashion, not unlike the anemonefishes (*Amphiprion*). Their striking patterns gradually fade with increased growth, and the adults of most species are relatively drab. The common appellation "sweetlips" is derived from the large, blubbery lips that are typical for the genus.

# Chapter Thirteen

# *Goatfishes*

Goatfishes of the family Mullidae are easily recognized by their distinctive shape and behavior, and especially by the presence of a pair of elongate barbels or "whiskers" on the chin. The barbels are special sensory organs that are used as "fingers" to probe the sandy bottom for various food items, including gastropods, pelecypods, and polychaete worms. During this activity a significant amount of sand is ingested. Crabs, shrimps, and small fishes also form a substantial part of the goatfish diet.

The family has a circumtropical distribution, but the vast majority of species inhabit the Indo-West Pacific region. Three genera are found there including *Parupeneus* (about 12 species), *Upeneus* (about 10 species), and *Mulloidichthys* (3 species). The genus *Upeneichthys* is endemic to the southern Australia-New Zealand region. All are similar in general morphology, being characterized by a rather slender body, two separate dorsal fins, and of course the presence of barbels. The members of *Upeneus* have teeth on the roof of the mouth and lack a small spine on the upper third of the gill margin, features that are contrary to *Parupeneus* and *Mulloidichthys*. The latter genera are separated from one another by dentition and the broader space between the two dorsal fins in *Mulloidichthys*. *Mulloidichthys* has a band of numerous fine teeth in the jaws and five scales between the two dorsals, in contrast to *Parupeneus*, which has a single row of relatively large teeth and only two or three scales between the dorsal fins.

Goatfishes are an integral part of the coral reef community. They are either solitary in habit or travel over the reef in pairs or small groups. They are usually encountered over sandy areas adjacent to reefs. During daylight hours they busily probe the sand in search of food, but at night they rest motionless on the bottom, often assuming a variegated color pattern that is quite different from the normal daytime pattern. Most species are relatively small, usually under 40 cm in length, but several, such as *Parupeneus chryserydros*, may reach more than 60 cm. The flesh is very tasty, and these fish are therefore highly prized by anglers and spear fishermen. In some localities they are caught in large numbers with traps and nets.

Goatfish spawning was observed recently in the Caribbean Sea by scientists from the University of Puerto Rico. A large group of 300-400 spotted goatfish (*Pseudupeneus maculatus*) engaged in spawning activities just prior to sunset. Usually three to seven individuals would break off from the main group and swim up a short distance above the bottom with their heads angled toward one another. They then quickly accelerated upward at a sharp angle for about one meter and simultaneously released eggs and sperm at the apex of the ascent. This spawning behavior is very similar to that reported for a number of wrasses and parrotfishes.

# Chapter Fourteen

# Symbiosis and Commensalism

One of the most interesting aspects of the coral reef community involves partnerships formed between different species of fishes or between a fish and an invertebrate organism. If the association is beneficial in some way to both partners the relationship is commonly referred to as *symbiosis*. On the other hand, *commensalism* is a term often used for a relationship in which only one of the two animals obtains some sort of advantage. Common examples of commensalism are the relationships that exist between remoras or sharksuckers and larger marine fishes, especially sharks and rays. The dorsal fin of the remora is specially modified to form a sucking apparatus that is used for attachment to the host. The remora benefits by saving energy due to its limited swimming and obtains food scraps when its host is feeding. Another classic example is the association existing between the man-of-war fishes (Nomeidae) that congregate among the deadly tentacles of jellyfish. This behavior enables them to escape larger predators. Certain jacks (Carangidae) exhibit this behavior only during their youth. The relationship is terminated when they attain a sufficient size and degree of mobility to render them less vulnerable.

Perhaps the best documented case of symbiosis is the one involving the anemonefishes of the genus *Amphiprion* (Pomacentridae) that dwell among the tentacles of tropical sea anemones. The latter animals are capable of stinging most fishes, but the anemonefishes possess a special mucous coating that somehow prevents the discharge of the anemone's stinging cells. Both partners apparently benefit from the relationship. The fish is protected from predators by the stinging cells and the anemone, in turn, is guarded against anemone-eating fishes by its highly territorial fish occupants. The anemonefishes also keep the surface of their host free of silt and other debris, and it has been suggested that they also serve as decoys that lure fishes into the deadly tentacles of the anemone, thus providing the anemone's food. However, studies in nature indicate that this does not occur. Most of the large tropical anemones feed mainly on plankton that is swept into the tentacles by the currents. Another fallacy involves the deliberate feeding of the anemone by the fish occupants. This behavior is easily induced in aquarium surroundings but rarely is seen in nature.

A symbiotic relationship similar to that of anemones and damselfishes is seen between tiny clingfishes of the genus *Lepadichthys* (Gobiesocidae) and tropical comasteroid crinoids, commonly known as sea lilies. The fish is remarkably well camouflaged and uses the tentacles of the crinoid for shelter. Also it probably utilizes the planktonic food that adheres to the sticky tentacles of its host. Crinoids provide concealment for several other small reef animals including shrimps, crabs, and brittle stars.

Another well known case of symbiosis involves wrasses of the genus *Labroides* and other members of the reef fish community. The wrasses or cleanerfishes feed upon the external parasites and diseased or damaged tissues of other fishes, thus providing a beneficial health service. Studies in which cleanerfishes have been experimentally removed from a section of reef resulted in significant increases in parasitism and disease. The cleaners are very meticulous with their inspections, often entering the mouth or gills of voracious predators such as groupers, snappers, and moray eels with total impunity. The shrimp genus *Stenopus* and several other fishes, most notably the young of wrasses, butterflyfishes, and angelfishes, also sometimes serve as ectoparasite cleaners.

# Chapter Fifteen

# *Butterflyfishes and Allies*

Of all the reef's inhabitants, no other fish family commands the popularity of the handsome butterflyfishes. Long admired by scientists, sport divers, photographers, and aquarists, the noble members of the family Chaetodontidae are renowned for their panoply of multi-hued color patterns. The family is represented worldwide by 113 species that are found primarily on coral reefs, although a few are mainly confined to subtropical or warm temperate seas. Most are relatively small in stature (maximum length usually under 25 cm) and are characterized by a compressed body with stout dorsal and anal spines. Typically they are confined to isolated patch reefs or limited sections of larger reefs at depths less than 15-20 m, but a few species penetrate greater depths. By day they roam widely within the confines of the "home range" in search of food, which consists of hard and soft corals, algae, small benthic invertebrates (other than corals, for example crabs and shrimps), planktonic animals, or a combination of these items. Some species, for example those belonging to the genera *Chelmon* and *Forcipiger*, have evolved an elongate snout that is effectively employed to extract food from otherwise inaccessible reef crevices. A small number of species, including *Chaetodon trifascialis* and *C. triangulum*, are highly territorial and solitarily defend one or more large heads of plate coral (*Acropora*) against intruding members of the same species or other coral-feeding butterflyfishes. Many chaetondontids form male–female pairs that roam the reef together, and there are strong indications that in some species these pairs are permanent. Members of the genus *Hemitaurichthys*, *Heniochus diphreutes*, and a few *Chaetodon* species form aggregations of up to

several hundred individuals that feed on plankton well above the bottom. There is little information on the reproductive habits of butterflyfishes. Apparently they produce small buoyant eggs that immediately float to the surface. The hatching time is estimated at one to two days with a temperature of approximately 29°C. The larvae are covered with bony plates and scientists refer to this stage as the "tholichthys." Although accurate information is non-existent, it appears that the pelagic larval stage lasts for periods ranging from a few weeks to several months.

The family is well represented on Indian Ocean-Red Sea reefs with 65 species belonging to eight genera. *Chaetodon*, with 48 species, is by far the largest genus. Seven species (*C. austriacus*, *C. fasciatus*, *C. larvatus*, *C. mesoleucos*, *C. paucifasciatus*, *C. semilarvatus*, and *Heniochus intermedius*) are restricted to the Red Sea-Gulf of Aden. Others have relatively broad regional distributions, and at least 20 species range widely over most of the vast tropical Indo-Pacific from Hawaii to East Africa. The following species are representative of the latter category: *C. auriga*, *C. citrinellus*, *C. kleinii*, *C. lunula*, *C. lineolatus*, *C. trifascialis*, *C. trifasciatus*, *C. unimaculatus*, *Forcipiger flavissimus*, *Heniochus acuminatus*, and *H. diphreutes*.

The fishes of the family Scorpididae from the Australian region bear a superficial resemblance to the butterflyfishes and some, for example *Tilodon sexfasciatum*, were formerly considered to be chaetodontids. The family contains fewer than one dozen species, of which the Stripey (*Microcanthus strigatus*) is the best known. Rudderfishes, family Kyphosidae, are close relatives of the scorpidids and are represented in the Indian Ocean by several species. Another Australian species greatly resembling a butterflyfish is the Old Wife *(Enoplosus armatus)*, the sole member of the family Enoplosidae. It inhabits weed-covered reefs along the southern margin of the island continent.

Members of the family Ephippidae are characteristically rounded in shape and strongly compressed laterally. The group is found on both Atlantic and Indo-Pacific reefs, with the latter area inhabited by about seven or eight species. *Drepane punctata* is a common species in the Indian Ocean, usually occurring over sandy areas. It is frequently among the catch of trawl fishermen. The best-known genus is *Platax*, the species of which are commonly known at batfishes. The four Indo-Pacific members of this genus grow to a moderately large size (about 50 cm) and are often encountered in large aggregations in the vicinity of coral reefs or in silty bays or harbors around piers or wreckage. Young specimens exhibit spectacularly elongated dorsal and anal fins and are highly prized as aquarium pets. With increased growth these fins become proportionately smaller in relation to overall body size.

Boarfishes (family Pentacerotidae) are mainly confined to warm temperate and subtropical reefs. There are approximately 11 known species that are confined to the western Pacific and Indian Oceans. They are frequently encountered in pairs near the entrances to caverns. The high dorsal fin and pig-like snout are unmistakable characters that help to distinguish these fishes.

# Chapter Sixteen

# *Angelfishes*

The angelfishes (family Pomacanthidae) are close relatives of the butterflyfishes, and until recently the two were usually classified in the same family. Angelfishes are easily separated from butterflyfishes by the presence of a stout backward-projecting spine on the lower edge of the cheek (preopercular bone). In addition, they lack the "armor-plated" tholichthys larval stage found in the butterflyfishes. Angelfishes occur in all tropical seas, but the great majority reside in the Indo-West Pacific. In the Indian Ocean 31 species belonging to six genera have been recorded. The two largest genera in this region are *Centropyge* and *Pomacanthus*, each represented by about 10-12 species. Angelfishes range in size from the diminutive pygmy angelfishes *(Centropyge)*, with a maximum length in some species of 8 cm or less, to the robust *Pomacanthus* angels that attain lengths of 40-50 cm. The latter genus is characterized by dramatic changes in color pattern associated with the various growth stages. The juveniles are so different from the adults that scientists in the last century generally considered them as separate species. The juveniles are secretive dwellers of dark caverns and ledges, and although adults share this habitat to a certain extent they frequently make forays into the open. Large *Pomacanthus* adults sometimes produce a loud thumping noise that is capable of startling an unsuspecting diver. Angelfishes are conspicuous elements of the shallow reef fauna. They frequent areas of dense coral, rocky ledges, and rubble slopes. Most live above 30 meters depth, but a few *Centropyge* and *Genicanthus* species penetrate to at least 70 meters. Angelfishes have small, numerous, bristle-like teeth and feed on a wide variety of items. Some species of *Centropyge* feed almost exclusively on algae, whereas *Pomacanthus*, *Chaetodontoplus*, and *Pygoplites* mainly eat sponges supplemented with algae, zoantharians, tunicates, and gorgonians. The *Genicanthus* angels form midwater aggregations that feed on plankton. The members of this genus exhibit pronounced sexual differences in color pattern, and males possess a more strongly forked caudal fin.

Some *Centropyge* and *Genicanthus* species typically occur in harems composed of a single dominant male and several females, the latter exhibiting a "pecking order" or hierarchical system of dominance among themselves. These groups appear to be more or less permanent, and if the male is experimentally removed the top-ranking female gradually transforms into the male sex and assumes control of the group. During courtship there is much rapid swimming by the male, accompanied by displays in which the fins are fully extended. Eventually the female approaches at close range and is "nuzzled" around the abdomen by the male, which leads to a sudden upward spawning rush resulting in the release of the gonadal products in open water. The male generally spawns with each female member of the harem during the session, which lasts about 10 minutes and occurs at dusk. Unlike *Centropyge* and *Genicanthus*, the *Pomacanthus*, *Chaetodontoplus*, and *Pygoplites* angels appear to form monogamous pairs, but there is little information available on their spawning habits.

## Chapter Seventeen

# *The Reef at Night*

As night descends upon the reef the diurnal fishes, those that are active during daylight, gradually retire to shelter on the bottom. At the same time various species that remain concealed by day emerge from the shadows to begin their nocturnal foraging activities. Although generally there are not nearly as many reef fishes apparent during the hours of darkness, diving at night is a rewarding experience and gives a very different perspective regarding the composition of the reef community. Many species that form tight aggregations in caverns during the day, for example squirrelfishes (Holocentridae), cardinalfishes (Apogonidae), sweeps (Pempheridae), and bigeyes (Priacanthidae), are widely dispersed in open water after nightfall. They feed on a myriad of small fishes and invertebrates. Moray eels (Muraenidae) appear to be equally active day or night. Apparently they will seize suitable prey whenever the opportunity arises no matter what the time of day. On the contrary, the snake eels (Ophichthidae) usually remain concealed during the day and are active mainly at night. They are often encountered on sand bottoms during this time.

Perhaps the most noteworthy of nocturnal reef species are the amazing flashlight fishes of the family Anomalopidae. They have a special luminous organ just below the eye producing a bright light that can be blinked on and off. The light is actually produced by bacteria that live in the sac-like organs. Apparently the lights are used to see by, for communication, to lure prey, and to confuse predators. There are two types of flashlight fishes, *Anomalops*, with two dorsal fins, and *Photoblepharon*, with a single dorsal.

A scientific study conducted several years ago on the Great Barrier Reef of Australia revealed that there is a more or less orderly sequence of retirement at dusk among the diurnal fishes. In other words, certain groups of fishes cease their foraging activities and settle onto the bottom for the night at different times. They apparently receive their cue from the intensity of prevailing light because retirement times are significantly earlier on overcast days. According to this study the wrasses (Labridae) are the first to disappear, with most species burying themselves in the sand. They are followed by small schooling damselfishes (Pomacentridae), with butterflyfishes (Chaetodontidae) retiring next followed by surgeonfishes (Acanthuridae) and rabbitfishes (Siganidae). The parrotfishes (Scaridae) are next, and the last to retire are the larger, solitary damselfishes. This order is more or less reversed at dawn when the fishes emerge from their resting places.

After nightfall the various diurnal species remain motionless in a state that approaches human sleep. Their metabolism is significantly lowered and response to external stimuli such as a spotlight or light touch is sluggish. Many colorful reef fishes are easy to catch at this time, and professional aquarium collectors take full advantage of this behavior.

Special night color patterns are assumed by a host of species including Moorish Idols, butterflyfishes, damselfishes, surgeonfishes, rabbitfishes, and fusiliers (Caesionidae). Typically the colors are less vivid than those exhibited during daylight hours.

# Chapter Eighteen

# *Damselfishes*

The damselfishes (Pomacentridae) form one of the largest families inhabiting tropical inshore waters. Their interesting behavior and ecological diversity are responsible for a large following among diving scientists, and consequently an impressive list of publications on this group has resulted over the past decade. Bright color patterns, small size, and quick acclimation to captivity are features that make them equally attractive to aquarists. Damselfishes inhabit all tropical and warm temperate seas. There are an estimated 300 species belonging to 22 genera. The majority of species inhabit the Indo-Pacific region, and to date about 100 species and 18 genera have been recorded from the Indian Ocean. Pomacentrids dwell in a wide variety of habitats including brackish mangrove estuaries, silty harbors and bays, tidal pools, rocky shores, weed and sand flats, rubble areas, and rich living coral reefs. A few species are known to occasionally enter fresh water. The majority of tropical species are restricted to relatively narrow habitat zones that are best defined on the basis of depth and substrate conditions. For example, some members of the genus *Chrysiptera* dwell on shallow reef flats, often in areas of breaking surf. Others, including most *Amblyglyphidodon* and *Paraglyphidodon*, are usually associated with rich hard and soft coral growth at depths below the influence of waves. A few species, particularly in the genus *Chromis*, are restricted to relatively deep water, between about 20 and 80 meters or more. The species of Indian Ocean anemonefishes (genus *Amphiprion*) are symbiotic with large tropical sea anemones. They are among the most colorful members of the damselfish family.

Well over half of the Indian Ocean representatives of this family belong to the largest genera: *Chromis, Pomacentrus, Stegastes,* and *Abudefduf*. There are many exceptions, but the drab brownish or blackish species, for example those belonging to *Stegastes* and *Pomacentrus*, tend to be benthic algal feeders in contrast to the more colorful species that forage at least partially on plankton. Many damselfishes, for example *Amphiprion, Abudefduf,* and a number of *Pomacentrus* and *Chrysiptera* species, are omnivorous, feeding primarily on planton, algae, and small benthic invertebrates. Most species of *Chromis* dwell on the outer or seaward reef slope and in passes where currents are strong. They form huge schools that feed on plankton high above the bottom.

Most benthic-dwelling pomacentrids are highly territorial and zealously guard a small plot (one or two square meters) of turf against other algal-feeding fishes including conspecifics. This territoriality is further enhanced during reproductive periods. The spawning behavior of damselfishes is highly stereotyped and is usually preceded by nest preparation and courtship. The latter includes rapid up and down swimming by the male, sometimes termed "signal-jumping," that serves to attract gravid females to the nest site. Depending on the species, between about 100 and 1000 eggs are deposited on firm bottom material, often rock or coral. The eggs are oval to cylindrical in shape and are attached to the substrate by numerous adhesive filaments. Hatching occurs in a few days to one week, and in most species the nest is carefully guarded by the male or both parents throughout the incubation period. The parents fan the eggs with their pectoral fins to keep them free of debris and also remove dead or diseased eggs by mouth. Certain wrasses and butterflyfishes are ravenous egg-eaters, and their presence in the vicinity of the nest triggers a strong aggressive reaction (from the male parent in particular). The young are pelagic for several weeks after hatching and eventually settle on shallow reefs where they assume the typical juvenile coloration. In many species the youthful livery includes a dark spot or ocellus ("false" eye-spot) on the dorsal fin. This mark usually disappears with increased growth but persists into adulthood in some species.

## Chapter Nineteen

# *Hawkfishes and Allies*

The hawkfishes of the family Cirrhitidae are small, colorful inhabitants of tropical reefs from shallow wave-swept limestone flats to depths of at least 50 fathoms. They are bottom-dwelling fishes that closely resemble certain serranids and are characterized by a single notched dorsal fin with the membranes deeply incised between each dorsal spine. Other characters include thickened lower pectoral rays that are unbranched, a fringe of epidermal filaments or cirri on the hind edge of the anterior nostril, and usually similar filaments present near the tip of each dorsal spine. The common name "hawkfish" is derived from their habit of perching on coral ledges, which is reminiscent of the behavior of their avian namesakes. From these reef look-outs they make quick periodic feeding dashes, seizing various prey items consisting mainly of small fishes and crustaceans. The thickened lower pectoral rays probably represent an adaptation that aids the support of these bottom-dwellers.

All but three of the 35 known species are found in the Indo-West Pacific; 17 of these inhabit Indian Ocean reefs. Species such as *Cirrhitus pinnulatus, Oxycirrhitus typus, Paracirrhites forsteri,* and *P. arcuatus* are widely distributed throughout the Indo-Pacific, while others, for example *Cirrhitichthys guichenoti* of Mauritius and Reunion, are restricted to small islands. This last mentioned species is considered to be extremely rare and the photo that appears here is (as far as known) the only one in existence taken in the natural habitat.

The shallow-dwelling *Paracirrhites hemistictus* exhibits two very different adult color phases that seem unrelated to sex. It is possible that the color phases are influenced by different habitat conditions although further study is needed. Most species of hawkfish are too small to be of value as food fishes, but they make excellent aquarium pets. One species in particular, the Long-nosed Hawkfish, commands a high price and is sought after by aquarists because of its unusual shape and vivid coloration. They are relatively rare in the aquarium trade because of their deep-dwelling habits, being most abundant in black coral thickets at depths between about 15 and 50 fathoms.

The Cheilodactylidae (morwongs) and Aplodactylidae (sea carps) are families related to the hawkfishes that are confined mainly to the temperate seas of the Australia–New Zealand region, although cheilodactylids are also present at other subtropical localities including Hawaii, Easter Island, Japan, and southern Africa. They are generally larger in size than the hawkfishes, with some species reaching 80 cm and valued as food. They inhabit rocky reefs and are similar to hawkfishes with regard to body shape and general behavior, spending much of the time resting on the bottom. There are approximately 20 species in the family Cheilodactylidae, with the majority of species included in the genus *Cheilodactylus* (*Goniistius* is a junior synonym). Other genera include *Nemadactylus* and *Dactylophora* of Australia-New Zealand and *Chirodactylus* of southern Africa. *Dactylosargus arctidens,* the sea carp of New Zealand and southern Australia, is the sole member of the family Aplodactylidae that enters the Indian Ocean.

# Chapter Twenty

# *Feeding Habits*

The coral reef and its adjacent waters provide a home for a seemingly endless variety of plants and animals. The members of the reef community are highly dependent on one another for food. Their complex feeding interactions are sometimes referred to as a food web; the web in turn is divided into several categories known as trophic levels. The food web (or food chain) can be thought of as consisting of at least four distinct trophic levels. The first level contains the plants, particularly various algae, which are primary producers directly utilizing the sun's energy to manufacture living tissue through the process of photosynthesis. The overall plant biomass, the total amount of living plant tissue in a particular community (including current-borne phytoplankton), greatly exceeds that of the higher trophic levels. There is generally a decrease in biomass and decreased potential for energy proceeding from one trophic level to the next. At first glance there appear to be only minimal amounts of algae present on most coral reefs and it would appear that the biomass of coral must certainly be greater. However, a special type of symbiotic algae known as zooxanthellae is contained within the tissues of the corals. This type of algae combined with filamentous algae growing in the pores of the dead coral skeletons account for a significant portion of the plant biomass.

The second trophic level consists of organisms commonly known as herbivores that feed directly on plant matter. These animals are the most efficient ones in terms of energy utilization, and their overall biomass exceeds that of the omnivores and carnivores occupying the higher trophic levels. The most important groups of herbivorous reef fishes include the mullets (Mugilidae), parrotfishes (Scaridae), surgeonfishes (Acanthuridae), rabbitfishes (Siganidae), rudderfishes (Kyphosidae), and certain butterflyfishes (Chaetodontidae), damselfishes (Pomacentridae), blennies (Blenniidae), triggerfishes (Balistidae), filefishes (Monacanthidae), boxfishes (Ostraciontidae), and puffers (Tetraodontidae). These algal-feeders can be divided into grazers and browsers. The first group crop their food very close to the bottom, sometimes ingesting part of the substrate as well. It includes such fishes as the surgeons, damsels, blennies, and triggers. Browsers have cutting teeth adapted for biting off bits of fronds or filaments above the reef surface. This group also includes members of the same families that exhibit grazing habits.

The third trophic level includes mainly small carnivores that feed on tiny zooplankton, small fishes, and invertebrates. Some common reef fishes that occupy this level are the damselfishes of the genus *Chromis*, lizardfishes (Synodontidae), moray eels (Muraenidae), squirrelfishes (Holocentridae), cardinalfishes (Apogonidae), groupers (Serranidae), snappers (Lutjanidae), wrasses (Labridae), and a host of other groups.

The fourth trophic level is occupied primarily by the larger predatory fishes, including sharks, moray eels, jacks (Carangidae), tunas (Scombridae), barracudas (Sphyraenidae), etc. These are discussed in more detail later. The higher trophic levels also include omnivorous fishes, species that feed on both plants and small animals. Important species in this category include some damselfishes, parrotfishes, gobies, wrasses, triggerfishes, and puffers.

# Chapter Twenty-one

# *Wrasses*

The wrasse family Labridae is certainly one of the most successful groups of reef fishes in terms of their overall diversity. They exhibit a wide range of shapes, colors, behaviors, and habitat preferences. The family is well represented in all tropical and temperate seas, but the vast majority of species are inhabitants of the Indo-Pacific region. In the Indian Ocean alone there are an estimated 120 species belonging to some 27 genera. They range in maximum adult size from just a few centimeters to more than two meters. Most species are relatively elongate in shape and somewhat laterally flattened. There is normally a single dorsal fin (except in some *Xyrichthys*) and the teeth tend to be conical, sometimes enlarged and tusk-like. Wrasses are generally omnivorous. Their diet contains such items as crabs, shrimps, starfishes, sea urchins, small fishes, gastropods, polychaetes, zooplankton, and algae. Members of the genus *Thalassoma* are particularly fond of demersal fish eggs, especially those of damselfishes. The majority of wrasses tend to be solitary in habit or form small groups that are confined to a certain section of a particular reef. Members of the genera *Cirrhilabrus* and *Paracheilinus*, however, form large schools that feed on plankton high above the bottom.

The tropical wrasses are noted for their bright colors. Many species show rather dramatic changes in color pattern that are correlated with growth and sex. This phenomenon is particularly well developed in the genus *Coris*, and several examples of its remarkable variation are illustrated here. Most labrids that have been investigated are characterized by female to male sex-reversal. This trait is often influenced by group social behavior. Some wrasses, for example species of *La-broides* and *Cirrhilabrus*, band together in "harems" with a single dominant male and several females. If anything happens to the male (for example if eaten by a predator) a gradual transformation occurs in the highest ranking (i.e., most aggressive) female. Her ovaries transform into testes and the bright colors of the male are assumed.

Wrasses of the genera *Cheilinus* and *Choerodon* are common in coral reef areas. They are among the largest reef dwellers. The Undulate Wrasse (*Cheilinus undulatus*) grows to over two meters with a weight of several hundred pounds. It is sometimes referred to as the Truck Wrasse because of its enormity. Although labrids are commonly used as food fish, the flesh is generally not of a high caliber. However, some species of *Choerodon* are exceptionally tasty.

Wrasses occur in virtually every habitat zone on tropical reefs. Most species are found in relatively calm water in coral areas between about three and 20 meters. This is the stronghold of *Halichoeres*, which boasts more species than any other wrasse genus in the Indo-Pacific. Juveniles of a number of species may be found in surge pools of the intertidal zone, and the adults of several *Thalassoma* species prefer shallow wave-swept reef flats and rocky shores. The razor wrasses of the genera *Cymolutes*, *Novaculichthys*, and *Xyrichthys* are inhabitants of barren sand flats. They elude predators by diving head first beneath the sand and are able to move quickly in any direction once buried. In similar fashion, many coral reef wrasses retire under a layer of sand during the night.

In recent years a number of undescribed wrasses have been discovered by diving scientists. Most of these were collected with the aid of SCUBA gear at depths greater than 20 meters. Because of their deep-dwelling habits they had escapted notice. Some coral reef wrasses penetrate to depths of at least 75-80 meters, well below the zone of routine diving. The majority of new discoveries belong to the genera *Bodianus*, *Cirrhilabrus*, *Halichoeres*, and *Paracheilinus*.

The breeding behavior of wrasses has been the subject of numerous scientific articles. Most species that have been investigated exhibit similar spawning patterns. Group spawning is common. Males perform a courtship "dance" that attracts one or more females. The actual spawning sequence involves a quick burst of rapid swimming toward the surface followed by an abrupt return to the bottom. Eggs and sperm are simultaneously released at the apex of the ascent. Behaviorally speaking, two of the most noteworthy genera are *Epibulus* and *Labroides*. The former genus contains a single species (*E. insidiator*) that feeds by everting its jaws, thus forming a peculiar telescopic tube that presumably is useful for probing hard-to-reach fissures in the reef. The species of *Labroides*, cleanerfishes, are well known for their habit of feeding on the external parasites and damaged tissues of reef fishes. Their "fish service stations" are located at more or less regular intervals over the reef and are vital to the overall health of the fish community.

# Chapter Twenty-two

# *Predators of the Reef*

The predatory fishes of the coral reef range widely in size and shape from tiny sea whip gobies that catch planktonic animals to the large, ferocious sharks and barracudas that are capable of seizing larger, more mobile prey. In this chapter we illustrate a few of the more or less conspicuous members of the predator community. At first glance the sandy verges of the reef resemble barren desert sands lapping against an oasis. Certainly the majority of fishes prefer the shelter of coral thickets. However, a number of small species, particularly juveniles, abound in the zone where reef meets sand or around rubble enclaves in the midst of vast sandy flats. These areas are exploited by a number of well-camouflaged fish predators including flatfishes (Bothidae, Soleidae, etc.), flatheads (*Platycephalus*), lizardfishes (Synodontidae), and snake eels (Ophichthidae). The crocodile snake eel (*Brachysomophis crocodilinus*) conceals itself below the surface of the sand with only the eyes and snout protruding. When suitable prey in the form of a small fish or crustacean passes within striking distance, it is summarily devoured.

Vast silvery shoals of small herrings, sardines, and silversides form an integral part of the reef fish community. They provide an abundant food source for the slender needle-fishes (Belonidae), halfbeaks (Hemiramphidae), and flyingfishes (Exocoetidae) that dwell in surface waters. The body color of these predators is countershaded light ventrally and dark dorsally, which makes them less visible to both bird predators from above and larger fish predators from below. It is also probably useful in avoiding detection by the smaller fishes that they themselves prey upon.

The largest reef predators include the sharks, barracudas (Sphyraenidae), jacks (Carangidae), snappers (Lutjanidae), and groupers (Serranidae). To chase down smaller fishes they rely on speed generated by powerful swimming muscles. Although relatively few in number compared to the myriad of small reef creatures, they represent an element of the reef fauna most often noticed by amateur divers, fishermen, and reef tourists in general. All of these groups, with the possible exception of sharks (which although tasty are not often eaten in the tropics), are coveted as food and game fishes. The tunas are mainly inhabitants of the high seas, but a few species, including the two-meter-long Dog-tooth Tuna (*Gymnosarda unicolor*), roam extensive territories in the immediate vicinity of coral reefs.

# Chapter Twenty-three

# *Parrotfishes*

Parrotfishes (family Scaridae) are one of the most conspicuous elements of the coral reef community. Like the closely related wrasses, they are characterized by bright color patterns that, in particular species, go through a series of rather dramatic changes during the life cycle. Juveniles and females generally have a relatively drab coloration consisting mainly of browns, greens, tans, or gray, sometimes with a reddish suffusion. Mature females are capable of transformation to the male sex and during this process undergo a remarkable color change. Males typically exhibit bright color combinations of red, pink, green, and blue.

Parrotfishes derive their common name from the fused jaw teeth that are reminiscent of a parrot's beak. However, a few species have separate teeth. Their dentition and powerful jaw muscles are especially well adapted for scraping the algal turf from the limestone bottom. They also forage on living coral polyps and the associated zooxanthellae, a special type of algae found in the tissues of living corals. Many parrotfishes feed in large schools composed of one or more species. In addition, they often mix with surgeonfishes and other herbivores. While grazing, they ingest large amounts of calcareous material along with the algae and live coral polyps. This is ground into a fine powder with the pharyngeal teeth and subsequently voided with the feces. In this way they contribute substantially to the formation of bottom sediments.

Parrotfishes occur in all tropical and subtropical seas, but the great majority inhabit coral reefs of the Indian and western Pacific Oceans. Because of the wealth of species in this vast area and the presence in a single species of two or more color patterns associated with growth and sex, there is a great deal of confusion surrounding their identity. It is estimated that there are about 40-50 species in the Indian Ocean, most of which belong to the genus *Scarus*. The family is characterized by a bluntly rounded head, the unique dentition, and relatively large scales. Most species attain a maximum length of about 70 cm or less, but the Humphead Parrot *Bolbometopon muricatus* grows to 120 cm and a weight of about 80 kilograms. Parrotfishes are used for food although the flesh is overly soft and often has a strong "fishy" flavor. Only small juveniles are suitable for home aquarium pets, but most are unattractive in their young stages. One exception is the brilliant orange and white young of *Cetoscarus bicolor*, which is a popular aquarium fish.

The reproductive behavior of parrotfishes is very similar to that of wrasses. Spawning is characterized by a rapid rush toward the surface by a single male closely followed by the female partner. The gonadal products are released at the apex of the ascent and the spawners quickly retreat to the bottom. The small, spherical eggs float to the surface, and after hatching the larvae are dispersed to distant reefs by waves and currents.

# Chapter Twenty-four

# *Grubfishes*

The grubfishes, family Mugiloididae (sometimes referred to as Parapercidae), are an assemblage of elongated bottom-dwelling fishes that are common on reefs of the tropical Indo-Pacific region. Several species also inhabit cooler temperate waters, particularly around Japan and southern Australia. Most species are residents of sand or rubble and are somewhat drably colored, displaying various shades of brown, tan, or white, often with an overlying pattern of dark brown or blackish bars, stripes, or spots. Many species frequent relatively shallow reefs, but a few are restricted to deeper water, never venturing above 20 or 30 meters. Specimens from deep reefs and off-shore trawling grounds are often reddish or pink in color. Of the 32 known species inhabiting the Indo-West Pacific, about 15 are found in the tropical Indian Ocean. In addition, several species new to science have been discovered recently and still await formal description. Virtually all of the tropical reef and trawl-ground species are included in a single genus, *Parapercis*. Grubfishes are generally solitary in habit or sometimes occur in pairs. Their diet is basically a carnivorous one consisting mainly of shrimps and crabs or occasionally small fishes. The grubfishes are passive predators that spend long periods lying motionless on the bottom. They often perch on top of rocks or low coral outcrops.

# Chapter Twenty-five

# *Blennies and Triplefins*

The blennies (family Blenniidae) are small, elongated, bottom-dwelling fishes that occur worldwide on most tropical and subtropical reefs. The group is well represented in the Indian Ocean, with an estimated 80 species belonging to 30 genera. They are primarily shallow-water inhabitants, although some species of *Ecsenius* penetrate to depths of 30 meters or more. Blennies of the genus *Omobranchus* have their greatest abundance in mangrove estuaries and on silty dead reefs close to shore. Perhaps the best known genera are *Entomacrodus*, *Cirripectes*, and *Istiblennius*, which are well represented in the intertidal zone. These fishes are sometimes referred to as rock skippers because of their habit of skittering across the rocks from pool to pool between breaking waves. They are often seen resting completely out of water for short periods, leading some uninformed laymen to believe they are capable of breathing air. However, like most telosts they are equipped with gills and are dependent on water for their respiratory needs. Perhaps the most colorful of the reef-dwelling blennies are the members of the genus *Ecsenius*, represented by about ten Indian Ocean—Red Sea species. They are most common in rich coral reef areas.

Among the most interesting reef-dwellers are the sabertooth blennies, aptly named for their possession of a pair of enlarged, dagger-like canine teeth in the lower jaw. These are used for defensive purposes and intraspecific fighting. In the genus *Meiacanthus* these teeth are grooved and associated with venom glands. Experiments by scientists have shown that the poisonous bite of this fish is effective in discouraging predators. Apparently this is the reason why a number of different fish species have evolved color patterns and shapes

that effectively mimic the *Meiacanthus* blennies. Although they are not toxic they command the same respect as *Meiacanthus* from potential predators. Additional details on this type of mimicry were provided earlier. Unlike most blennies that are bottom-dwellers scurrying among the nooks and crannies of the reef, the sabertooth blennies are free swimmers that spend most of their time in midwater a short distance above the bottom. However, they may retire to holes in the reef at nightfall or when frightened and during reproductive activity. Blennies feed on a wide variety of food items, with algae comprising the bulk of the diet for many species. Other foods include tiny gastropods and crustaceans, foraminifera, and precipitated detritus. The sabertooth blennies of the genera *Aspidontus* and *Plagiotremus* feed largely on scales, fin membranes, and bits of flesh that are ripped from passing fishes during quick darting attacks. Members of the former genus effectively mimic the cleaner wrasse *Labroides* and are thus able to gain easy access to the naive youthful stages of many reef species. After a few attacks, however, the victims learn to differentiate between the true cleaners and *Aspidontus* and learn to avoid the latter.

The eel blennies (Congrogadidae) are a related family represented by only a few species on Indian Ocean coral reefs. *Congrogadus subducens* inhabits northern Australian reefs. Although it grows to a fair size (about 40 cm), it is seldom seen because of its shy and retiring habits.

The Tripterygiidae or triplefins are a family of blenny-like fishes characterized by three separate dorsal fins. There are numerous species inhabiting the Indo-Pacific region, but because of their very small size (most under 4 or 5 cm) they are inconspicuous dwellers of the reef surface. The largest Indian Ocean genus is *Enneapterygius* with at least 30 species, including many which are still undescribed. Most of the remaining species from this region belong to the genera *Helcogramma* or *Norfolkia*. These genera are most easily separated on the basis of scale characteristics. *Norfolkia* has a completely scaled head whereas the heads of the other two genera are scaleless. *Helcogramma* differs from *Enneapterygius* by having a continuous series of pored lateral-line scales which ends under the third dorsal fin, in contrast to a discontinuous lateral line consisting in its posterior part of a series of notched scales. The various species of triplefins often exhibit different male-female color patterns: males frequently show various shades of red, while females are often greenish. In several species of *Helcogramma* and *Enneapterygius* the males possess blackish coloration on the ventral portion of the head.

*Plates 1–144 and their accompanying captions follow.*
*Chapter 26 begins on page 220.*

# Captions to Plates 1–87

## PLATE 1

1-1. A sheltered reef at the Similan Islands, Andaman Sea.

1-2. Aerial view of Goss Passage and surrounding reefs, Houtman Abrolhos, Western Australia.

1-3. Vilingilli Island, South Male Atoll, Maldive Islands.

1-4. Dune formations along the Western Australian coast near Shark Bay.

1-5. Sheer cliffs and caves are characteristic shoreline features of Christmas Island.

1-6. Huge oceanic swells break along the eastern coast of Christmas Island.

## PLATE 2

2-1. A volcanic grotto at Christmas Island.

2-2. An aggregation of fairy basslets (*Anthias evansi*) on the precipitous outer reef slope at Christmas Island.

2-3. The authors at work on the outer reef slope of Christmas Island.

2-4. Soft corals in shallow water at Christmas Island.

## PLATE 3

3-1. Clear water and coral reefs abound at the Seychelles.

3-2. Exposed corals at low tide in Flying Fish Cove, Christmas Island.

3-3. A narrow platform of rich coral surrounds the coastline of Christmas Island. The fish is *Hemitaurichthys polylepis*, a member of the butterflyfish family.

3-4. Dead coral slabs litter the intertidal zone at Beacon Island, Houtman Abrolhos, Western Australia.

3-5. Fisherman under sail at Malindi, Kenya.

3-6. Victoria Harbor on the island of Mahe, Seychelles.

## PLATE 4

4-1. A big catch of carangid fishes at Mahe, Seychelles.

4-2. Arid mountains provide a scenic backdrop for the city of Mutrah, Oman.

4-3. Arab fisherman bring their catch ashore in the early morning at Khor Fakkan, Gulf of Oman. Fish traps used to catch reef-dwelling species can be seen in the foreground.

4-4. Spanish mackerel are the most important market fish at Muscat, Gulf of Oman.

4-5. A native of Sri Lanka slowly stalks a school of baitfish. Cast-nets of this type are commonly used throughout the Indo-Pacific region.

4-6. Arabian fish markets such as this one at Mutrah, Oman provide an interesting blend of modern and traditional life styles.

## PLATE 5

5-1. A trawl-net is slowly hauled aboard a government fishing vessel in the Gulf of Oman.

5-2. The result of a 30-minute tow in 40 m depth off Muscat, Gulf of Oman. Predominant among the catch are jacks, lethrinids, nemipterids, and lizardfishes.

5-3. The net bulges with a one-fourth ton catch.

5-4. Indian Ocean sunset.

## PLATE 6

6-1. Porpoise schools are a common sight throughout the Indian Ocean.

6-2. A green sea turtle in 16 m, Sodwana Bay, South Africa.

6-3. Expanded polyps of the golden coral (*Tubastrea aurea*), Similan Islands, Andaman Sea.

6-4. Zoanthid colony (*Zoanthus praelongus*), Lucky Bay, Western Australia.

6-5. A colony of anemones, Recherche Archipelago, Western Australia.

6-6. Algae, Lucky Bay, Western Australia.

## PLATE 7

7-1. Sponge cluster, Houtman Abrolhos, Western Australia.

7-2. Goblet sponges, Recherche Archipelago, Western Australia.

7-3. Flame red starfish (*Petricia vernicina*), Recherche Archipelago, Western Australia.

7-4. A scarlet sponge adorns the bottom at Goss Passage, Houtman Abrolhos, Western Australia.

7-5. Tightly coiled brittle star (*Astrobrachion*), on black coral, Mondrain Island, Recherche Archipelago, Western Australia.

7-6. Crinoids gain access to planktonic food by perching on sea whip stalks, Vilingilli, Maldive Islands.

## PLATE 8

8-1. Nudibranch on sponge, Cockburn Sound, Western Australia.

8-2. A well camouflaged spindle cowry (*Volva* sp.) laying eggs among the branches of a gorgonian, Phuket, Thailand.

8-3. A large octopus, Houtman Abrolhos, Western Australia.

8-4. Painted coral shrimp (*Hymenocera picta*), Mombasa, Kenya.

8-5. Coral shrimp (*Thor amboinensis*), a small (usually under 3 cm) species frequently found in association with sea anemones, Phuket, Thailand.

8-6. Western rock lobster (*Panulirus cygnus*), Cockburn Sound, Western Australia.

8-7. A hydrozoan (*Tubularia* sp.), Recherche Archipelago, Western Australia.

## PLATE 9

9-1. *Rhiniodon typus*, whale shark.

9-2. *Carcharodon carcharias*, white shark.

9-3. *Isurus oxyrinchus*, mako shark.

9-4. *Galeocerdo cuvieri*, tiger shark.

9-5. *Triaenodon obesus*, white-tip reef shark.

9-6. *Carcharhinus longimanus*, ocean white-tip shark.

9-7. *Carcharhinus amblyrhynchos*, grey reef shark.

9-8. *Carcharhinus melanopterus*, black-tip shark.

9-9. *Carcharhinus albimarginatus*, silver-tip shark.

9-10. *Negaprion acutidens*, lemon shark.

9-11a. *Stegostoma varium*, adult zebra shark.

9-11b. *Stegostoma varium*, juvenile zebra shark.

9-12. *Sphyrna lewini*, scalloped hammerhead.

9-13. *Sphyrna zygaena*, smooth hammerhead.

9-14. *Sphyrna lewini*, scalloped hammerhead.

## PLATE 10

10-1. *Rhyncobatus djeddensis*, guitarfish or shovelnose ray.

10-2. *Stoasodon narinari*, spotted eagle ray.

10-3. *Himantura uarnak*, coach-whip ray.

10-4. *Taeniura lymma*, blue-spot ray.

10-5. *Manta alfredi*, manta ray.

10-6. *Rhinoptera neglecta*, cow-nose ray.

10-7. *Taeniura melanospila*, black-spot ray.

10-8. *Torpedo marmoratus*, electric ray.

## PLATE 11

11-1. *Echidna nebulosa* (50 cm), Christmas Island, 4 m.

11-2. *Echidna nebulosa* (50 cm), Dampier Archipelago, Western Australia, 3 m.

11-3. *Enchelycore bayeri* (60 cm), Christmas Island, 8 m.

11-4. *Gymnothroax breedeni* (85 cm), Christmas Island, 15 m.

11-5. *Gymnothroax favagineus* (75 cm), Sodwana Bay, South Africa, 16 m.

11-6. *Siderea grisea* (60 cm), Mahe, Seychelles, 10 m.

11-7. *Gymnothorax javanicus* (150 cm), Vilingilli, Maldive Islands, 5 m.

PLATE 12

12-1. *Gymnothorax flavimarginatus* (70 cm), Vilingilli, Maldive Islands, 10 m.
12-2. *Gymnothorax flavimarginatus* (50 cm), Christmas Island, 10 m.
12-3. *Gymnothorax margaritophorus* (55 cm), Christmas Island, 8 m.
12-4. *Gymnothorax melatremus* (24 cm), Christmas Island, 20 m.
12-5. *Gymnothorax meleagris* (90 cm), Christmas Island, 12 m.
12-6. *Gymnothorax nudivomer* (90 cm), Sodwana Bay, South Africa, 28 m.
12-7. *Gymnothorax permistus* (75 cm), Colombo, Sri Lanka, 4 m.

PLATE 13

13-1. *Siderea picta* (70 cm), Coral Sea, 2 m.
13-2. *Gymnothorax tesselata* (100 cm), Shimoni, Kenya, 10 m.
13-3. *Gymnothorax undulatus*, juvenile phase (30 cm), Mauritius, 25 m.
13-4. *Gymnothorax* sp. (*G. flavimarginatus?*), adult (90 cm), Mauritius, 25 m.
13-5. *Gymnothorax zonipectus* (40 cm), Christmas Island, 10 m.
13-6. *Gymnothorax prasinus* (50 cm), Houtman Abrolhos, Western Australia, 10 m.
13-7. *Gymnothorax flavimarginatus* (50 cm), Gulf of Aqaba, Red Sea, 4 m.
13-8. *Enchelycore pardalis* (60 cm), Christmas Island, 10 m.

PLATE 14

14-1. *Rhinomuraena quaesita* (70 cm), Christmas Island, 25 m.
14-2. *Rhinomuraena quaesita* (70 cm), Rabaul, New Britain, 4 m.
14-3. *Myrichthys maculosus* (60 cm), Miyake Jima, Japan, 7m.
14-4. An unidentified eel, probably a heterocongrin (family Congridae).
14-5. *Brachysomophis crocodilinus* (120 cm), Christmas Island, 12m.
14-6. *Gorgasia maculata* (90 cm), Rabaul, New Britain, 5 m.
14-7. *Taenioconger haasi* (35 cm), Vilingilli, Maldive Islands, 40 cm.

PLATE 15

15-1. *Sargocentron diadema* (18 cm), Sodwana Bay, South Africa, 13 m.
15-2. *Sargocentron caudimaculatus* (15 cm), Vilingilli, Maldive Islands, 10 m.
15-3. *Sargocentron microstomus* (18 cm), Christmas Island, 12 m.
15-4. *Sargocentron spinifer* (30 cm), Vilingilli, Maldive Islands, 12 m.
15-5. *Sargocentron seychellensis* (18 cm), Mahe, Seychelles, 5 m.
15-6. *Sargocentron tiere* (24 cm), Christmas Island, 15 m.
15-7. *Neoniphon sammara* (20 cm), Vilingilli, Maldive Islands, 15 m.
15-8. *Neoniphon operculare.*

*PLATE 16*

16-1. *Myripristis adustus* (28 cm), Vilingilli, Maldive Islands, 8 m.
16-2. *Myripristis hexagonatus* (24 cm), Dampier Archipelago, Western Australia, 5 m.
16-3. *Myripristis kuntee* (20 cm), Trincomalee, Sri Lanka, 12 m.
16-4. *Myripristis melanostictus* (20 cm), Vilingilli, Maldive Islands, 30 m.
16-5. *Myripristis murdjan* (24 cm), Mahe, Seychelles, 12 m.
16-6. *Myripristis violaceus* (25 cm), Vilingilli, Maldive Islands, 6 m.
16-7. *Myripristis vittata* (23 cm), Christmas Island, 15 m.
16-8. *Myripristis adustus* and *M. vittata* sheltering in a rocky crevice.

PLATE 17

17-1. *Phycodurus eques* (15 cm), Recherche Archipelago, Western Australia, 10 m.
17-2. *Phyllopteryx taeniolatus* (23 cm), Recherche Archipelago, Western Australia, 10 m.
17-3. *Phycodurus eques* (35 cm), Recherche Archipelago, Western Australia, 10 m.
17-4. *Phyllopteryx taeniolatus* (23 cm), Recherche Archipelago, Western Australia, 10 m.
17-5. *Solenostomus armatus* (12 cm), Rabaul, New Britain, 5 m.
17-6. *Solenostomus cyanopterus* (20 cm), Mahe, Seychelles, 12 m.

## PLATE 18

18-1. *Corythoichthys amplexus* (12 cm), Mahe, Seychelles, 15 m.
18-2. *Corythoichthys haematopterus* (12 cm), Mahe, Seychelles, 8 m.
18-3. *Corythoichthys schultzi* (10 cm), Christmas Island, 12 m.
18-4. *Dunckerocampus multiannulatus* (15 cm), Mauritius, 10 m.
18-5. *Micrognathus spinirostris* (8 cm), North West Cape, Western Australia, 5 m.
18-6. *Hippocampus kuda* (9 cm), Cebu, Philippines, 3 m.
18-7. *Hippocampus angustus* (10 cm), Cockburn Sound, Western Australia, 5 m.

## PLATE 19

19-1. *Pterois antennata* (16 cm), Vilingilli, Maldive Islands, 12 m.
19-2. *Pterois antennata* (18 cm), Christmas Island, 10 m.
19-3. *Pterois volitans* (30 cm), Christmas Island, 6 m.
19-4. *Pterois volitans* (25 cm), Gulf of Aqaba, Red Sea, 6 m.
19-5. *Pterois radiata* (12 cm), Christmas Island, 10 m.

## PLATE 20

20-1. *Dendrochirus zebra* (20 cm), Christmas Island, 10 m.
20-2. *Dendrochirus brachypterus* (20 cm), Christmas Island, 10 m.
20-3. *Dendrochirus biocellatus* (15 cm), Rabaul, New Britain, 10 m.
20-4. *Taenianotus triacanthus* (12 cm), Rabaul, New Britain, 12 m.
20-5. *Taenianotus triacanthus*, family Scorpaenidae (12 cm), Rabaul, New Britain, 15 m. The leaf-fish is a well camouflaged member of the scorpionfish family. It periodically sheds its skin in reptilian fashion.
20-6. *Scorpaenodes steenei* (14 cm), Houtman Abrolhos, Western Australia, 10 m.
20-7. *Scorpaenodes parvipinnis* (6 cm), Mauritius, 5 m.

## PLATE 21

21-1. *Iracundus signifer* (10 cm), Mauritius, 25 m.
21-2. *Parascorpaena picta* (15 cm), Dampier Archipelago, Western Australia, 4 m.
21-3. *Sebastapistes cyanostigma* (7 cm), Christmas Island, 10 m.
21-4. *Scorpaena* sp. (22 cm), Houtman Abrolhos, Western Australia, 10 m.
21-5. *Scorpaenopsis* sp. (8 cm), Christmas Island, 10 m.
21-6. *Scorpaenopsis* sp. (20 cm), Christmas Island, 5 m.
21-7. *Scorpaenopsis* sp. (18 cm), Christmas Island, 5 m.
21-8. *Scorpaenopsis diabolis* (22 cm), Mauritius, 25 m.

## PLATE 22

22-1. *Synanceia alula* (25 cm), Great Barrier Reef (aquarium photo).
22-2. *Synanceia verrucosa* (30 cm), Mauritius, 25 m.
22-3. *Inimicus sinensis* (28 cm), Houtman Abrolhos, Western Australia, 20 m.
22-4. *Glyptauchen panduratus* (10 cm), Recherche Archipelago, Western Australia, 8 m.
22-5. *Perryena leucometopon* (12 cm), Recherche Archipelago, Western Australia, 8 m.
22-6. *Amblyapistus taenionotus* (12 cm), Guadalcanal, Solomon Islands, 5 m.
22-7. *Caracanthus maculatus* (4 cm), Christmas Island, 5 m.
22-8. *Caracanthus madagascariensis* (3 cm), Mombasa (aquarium photo).

## PLATE 23

23-1. *Amblyglyphidodon aureus* (13 cm), Similan Islands, Andaman Sea, 20 m.
23-2. *Amblyglyphidodon aureus* (14 cm), Christmas Island, 15 m.
23-3. *Plagiotremus rhinorhynchos* (10 cm), Vilingilli, Maldive Islands, 12 m.
23-4. *Plagiotremus rhinorhynchos* (10 cm), Great Barrier Reef, 10 m.
23-5. *Ecsenius bicolor* (6 cm), Christmas Island, 10 m.
23-6. *Ecsenius bicolor* (6 cm), Christmas Island, 15 m.
23-7. *Halichoeres hortulanus*, male (23 cm), Christmas Island, 10 m.
23-8. *Halichoeres hortulanus*, female (18 cm), Gulf of Aqaba, Red Sea, 10 m.

## PLATE 24

24-1. *Nemanthias carburyi*, male (10 cm), Vilingilli, Maldive Islands, 12 m.
24-2. *Nemanthias carburyi* (12 cm), Aliwal Shoal, South Africa, 10 m.
24-3. *Nemanthias carburyi*, female (6 cm), Shimoni, Kenya, 12 m.
24-4. *Anthias evansi*, male (14 cm), Vilingilli, Maldive Islands, 15 m.
24-5. *Anthias lori* (5 cm), Christmas Island, 35 m.

## PLATE 25

25-1. *Anthias kashiwae*, male (12 cm), Mauritius, 25 m.
25-2. *Anthias kashiwae*, female (8 cm), Shimoni, Kenya, 10 m.
25-3. *Anthias bicolor* (10 cm), Mauritius, 20 m.
25-4. *Anthias ignitus* (10 cm), Similan Islands, Andaman Sea, 15 m.
25-5. *Anthias* sp. (8 cm), Mauritius, 50 m.
25-6. *Anthias* sp. (8 cm), Rabaul, New Britain, 4 m.
25-7. *Anthias luzonensis*, male (10 cm), Great Barrier Reef, 40 m.
25-8. *Anthias luzonensis*, female (10 cm), Great Barrier Reef, 40 m.

## PLATE 26

26-1. *Anthias smithvanizi* (8 cm), Christmas Island, 40 m.
26-2. *Anthias dispar*, male (9 cm), Christmas Island, 12 m.
26-3. *Anthias squamipinnis*, male (12 cm), Vilingilli, Maldive Islands, 4 m.
26-4. *Anthias squamipinnis*, female (10 cm), Vilingilli, Maldive Islands, 4 m.
26-5. *Acanthistius pardalotus* (20 cm), Houtman Abrolhos, Western Australia, 15 m.
26-6. *Aethaloperca rogaa* (30 cm), Vilingilli, Maldive Islands, 6 m.
26-7. *Anyperodon leucogrammicus* (13 cm), Phuket, Thailand, 10 m.
26-8. *Anyperodon leucogrammicus* (25 cm), Vilingilli, Maldive Islands, 8 m.

## PLATE 27

27-1. *Gracila albomarginatus* (35 cm), Christmas Island, 20 m.
27-2. *Gracila polleni* (30 cm), Christmas Island, 35 m.
27-3. *Cephalopholis argus* (30 cm), Vilingilli, Maldive Islands, 5 m.
27-4. *Cephalopholis formosa* (25 cm), Phuket, Thailand, 5 m.
27-5. *Cephalopholis boenack* (18 cm), Phuket, Thailand, 5 m.
27-6. *Cephalopholis leoparda* (20 cm), Vilingilli, Maldive Islands, 8 m.
27-7. *Cephalopholis aurantia* (35 cm), Christmas Island, 30 m.
27-8. *Cephalopholis nigripinnis* (20 cm), Malindi, Kenya, 5 m.

## PLATE 28

28-1. *Cephalopholis miniata* (20 cm), Vilingilli, Maldive Islands, 25 m.
28-2. *Cephalopholis miniata* (30 cm), Vilingilli, Maldive Island, 20 m.
28-3. *Cephalopholis sexmaculata* (28 cm), Vilingilli, Maldive Islands, 15 m.
28-4. *Cephalopholis sonnerati* (50 cm), Coral Sea, 15 m.
28-5. *Cephalopholis sonnerati* (50 cm), North West Cape, Western Australia, 12 m.
28-6. *Cephalopholis urodela* (20 cm), Christmas Island, 12 m.
28-7. *Cephalopholis* sp. (14 cm), Vilingilli, Maldive Islands, 10 m.

## PLATE 29

29-1. *Epinephelides armatus* (10 cm), Recherche Archipelago, Western Australia, 10 m.
29-2. *Epinephelus caeruleopunctatus* (45 cm), Great Barrier Reef, 3 m.
29-3. *Epinephelus longispinis* (16 cm), Mahe, Seychelles, 10 m.
29-4. *Epinephelus fasciatus* (24 cm), Mahe, Seychelles, 10 m.
29-5. *Epinephelus fuscoguttatus* (35 cm), Vilingilli, Maldive Islands, 12 m.
29-6. *Epinephelus grammatophoros* (27 cm), Durban Aquarium, South Africa.
29-7. *Epinephelus hexagonatus* (30 cm), Mauritius, 6 m.
29-8. *Epinephelus rivulatus* (25 cm), Houtman Abrolhos, Western Australia, 10 m.

PLATE 30
30-1. *Epinephelus multinotatus* (40 cm), North West Cape, Western Australia, 12 m.
30-2. *Epinephelus summana* (25 cm), Vilingilli, Maldive Islands, 10 m.
30-3. *Cromileptes altivelis* (16 cm), Great Barrier Reef, 5 m.
30-4. *Dinoperca petersi* (38 cm), Sodwana Bay, South Africa, 28 m.
30-5. *Ellerkeldia wilsoni* (16 cm), Geographe Bay, Western Australia, 15 m.
30-6. *Luzonichthys microlepis* (6 cm), Christmas Island, 20 m.
30-7. *Othos dentex* (60 cm), Recherche Archipelago, Western Australia, 12 m.
30-8. *Belonoperca chabanaudi* (18 cm), Vilingilli, Maldive Islands, 8 m.

PLATE 31
31-1. *Variola louti* (7 cm), Vilingilli, Maldive Islands, 10 m.
31-2. *Variola louti* (60 cm), Vilingilli, Maldive Islands, 15 m.
31-3. *Plectropomus laevis* (13 cm), Mahe, Seychelles, 8 m.
31-4. *Plectropomus laevis* (70 cm), Great Barrier Reef, 5 m.
31-5. *Plectropomus leopardus* (65 cm), Houtman Abrolhos, Western Australia, 10 m.
31-6. *Pogonoperca punctata* (23 cm), Christmas Island, 30 m.
31-7. *Aulacocephalus temmincki* (30 cm), Miyake Jima, Japan, 20 m.
31-8. *Grammistes sexlineatus* (14 cm), Great Barrier Reef, 10 m.

PLATE 32
32-1. *Pseudochromis dutoiti* (7 cm), Sodwana Bay, South Africa, 2 m.
32-2. *Pseudochromis flavivertex* (7 cm), Jeddah, Red Sea, 5 m.
32-3. *Pseudochromis fridmani* (6 cm), Gulf of Aqaba, Red Sea, 5 m.
32-4. *Pseudochromis melas* (8 cm), Sodwana Bay, South Africa, 25 m.
32-5. *Labracinus lineatus* (20 cm), Houtman Abrolhos, Western Australia, 10 m.
32-6. *Glaucosoma hebraicum* (45 cm), Houtman Abrolhos, Western Australia, 16 m.
32-7. *Terapon jarbua* (12 cm), Kosi Bay, South Africa, 1 m.
32-8. *Kuhlia mugil* (12 cm), Kosi Bay, South Africa, 1 m.

PLATE 33
33-1. *Paraplesiops meleagris* (30 cm), Recherche Archipelago, Western Australia, 10 m.
33-2. *Calloplesiops altivelis* (10 cm), North West Cape, Western Australia (aquarium photo).
33-3. *Trachinops brauni* (6 cm), Recherche Archipelago, Western Australia, 18 m.
33-4. *Paraplesiops meleagris* (30 cm), Recherche Archipelago, Western Australia, 10 m.

PLATE 34
34-1. *Apogon angustatus* (8 cm), Christmas Island, 15 m.
34-2. *Apogon cyanosoma* (7 cm), Muscat, Oman, 5 m.
34-3. *Apogon robustus* (8 cm), Vilingilli, Maldive Islands, 5 m.
34-4. *Apogon robustus* (8 cm), Vilingilli, Maldive Islands, 8 m.
34-5. *Apogon taeniophorus* (8 cm), Kosi Bay, South Africa, 2 m.
34-6. *Apogon victoriae* (8 cm), Cockburn Sound, Western Australia, 5 m.
34-7. *Apogon fraenatus* (8 cm), Shimoni, Kenya, 8 m.
34-8. *Apogon nitidus* (7 cm), Mahe, Seychelles, 15 m.

PLATE 35
35-1. *Apogon apogonides* (8 cm), Christmas Island, 20 m.
35-2. *Apogon aureus* (10 cm), Christmas Island, 6 m.
35-3. *Apogon kallopterus* (10 cm), Mahe, Seychelles, 8 m.
35-4. *Apogon taeniatus* (8 cm), Mombasa, Kenya, 1 m.
35-5. *Apogon* sp. (6 cm), Phuket, Thailand, 4 m.
35-6. *Cheilodipterus quinquelineatus* (13 cm), Jeddah, Red Sea, 6 m.
35-7. *Cheilodipterus artus* (12 cm), Vilingilli, Maldive Islands, 5 m.
35-8. *Cheilodipterus lineatus* (16 cm), Vilingilli, Maldive Islands, 10 m.

## PLATE 36

36-1. *Archamia mossambica* (7 cm), Sodwana Bay, South Africa, 2 m.

36-2. *Sphaeramia orbicularis* (8 cm), Rabaul, New Britain, 6 m.

36-3. *Parapriacanthus ransonneti* (5 cm), Vilingilli, Maldive Islands, 20 m.

36-4. *Parapriacanthus ransonneti* (6 cm), Similan Islands, Andaman Sea, 12 m.

36-5. *Pempheris vanicolensis* (12 cm), Jeddah, Red Sea, 7 m.

36-6. *Pempheris vanicolensis* (14 cm), Mahe, Seychelles, 5 m.

36-7. *Pempheris oualensis* (12 cm), Mahe, Seychelles, 8 m.

36-8. *Ambassis commersoni* (5 cm), Kosi Bay, South Africa, 1 m.

## PLATE 37

37-1. *Paraluteres prionurus* (10 cm), Christmas Island, 12 m. This filefish is a near perfect mimic of the sharpnose puffer, *Canthigaster valentini*.

37-2. *Canthigaster valentini* (10 cm), Christmas Island, 15 m.

37-3. *Plagiotremus phenax* (8 cm), Vilingilli, Maldive Islands, 5 m. This species is an effective mimic of *Meiacanthus smithi*, another blenny.

37-4. *Meiacanthus smithi* (9 cm), Vilingilli, Maldive Islands, 5 m.

37-5. *Centropyge eibli* (11 cm), Christmas Island, 12 m.

37-6. *Acanthurus pyroferus* (10 cm), Similan Islands, Andaman Sea, 12 m. This juvenile is a mimic of *Centropyge eibli*.

37-7. *Lutjanus bohar*, juvenile (6 cm), Mahe, Seychelles, 8 m. The young of this snapper frequently mimic various *Chromis* (Pomacentridae) species. This individual was photographed among a school of *Chromis ternatensis*.

37-8. *Chromis ternatensis* (7 cm), Similan Islands, Andaman Sea, 3 m.

## PLATE 38

38-1. *Scorpaenopsis diabolus*, family Scorpaenidae (35 cm), Mauritius, 25 m.

38-2. *Scorpaenopsis* sp., family Scorpaenidae (25 cm), Christmas Island, 8 m.

38-3. *Iracundus signifer* (10 cm), Mauritius, 25 m. The dorsal fin of this scorpaenid resembles a small fish which is used as a decoy to attract prey. The bulging stomach of this individual is proof of the effectiveness of this unique luring divice.

38-4. *Scorpaenopsis* sp., family Scorpaenidae (18 cm), Malindi, Kenya, 7 m.

38-5. *Solenostomus cyanopterus*, family Solenostomidae (20 cm), Mahe, Seychelles, 10 m.

38-6 a-c. *Amblyapistus taenionotus*, family Scorpaenidae (12 cm), Great Barrier Reef, 4 m. This species effectively mimics a leaf as it rocks back and forth with the current.

## PLATE 39

39-1. *Platycephalus* sp., family Platycephalidae (24 cm), Phuket, Thailand, 10 m.

39-2. *Bothus mancus*, family bothidae (20 cm), Sodwana Bay, South Africa, 2 m.

39-3. *Samariscus triocellatus*, family Pleuronectidae (8 cm), Mauritius, 25 m.

39-4. *Cheilinus chlorurus*, family Labridae (14 cm), Mauritius, 2 m.

39-5. *Phycodurus eques*, family Syngnathidae (30 cm), Recherche Archipelago, Western Australia, 10 m. The appendages of the leafy sea dragon bear a close resemblance to kelp fronds.

## PLATE 40

40-1. *Carangoides chrysophrys*, longnose trevally.

40-2. *Carangoides ferdau*, blue trevally.

40-3. *Carangoides armatus*, longfin trevally.

40-4. *Carangoides malabaricus*, Malabar trevally.

40-5. *Caranx ignobilis*, giant trevally.

40-6. *Caranx lugubris*, black jack.

40-7. *Carangoides fulvoguttatus*, yellowspotted trevally.

40-8. *Caranx sexfasciatus*, bigeye trevally.

40-9. *Caranx melampygus*, bluefin trevally.

40-10. *Alectis indicus*, Indian threadfish.

40-11. *Decapterus russelli*, Indian scad.

40-12. *Atule mate*, yellowtail scad.

40-13. *Gnathanodon speciosus*, golden trevally.

40-14. *Elagatis bipinnulata*, rainbow runner.

## PLATE 41

41-1. *Megalaspis cordyla*, torpedo scad.
41-2. *Scomberoides commersonnianus*, Talang queenfish.
41-3. *Selar crumenophthalmus*, bigeye scad.
41-4. *Scomberoides tol*, needlescaled queenfish.
41-5. *Scomberoides lysan*, doublespotted queenfish.
41-6. *Selaroides leptolepis*, yellowstripe scad.
41-7. *Seriola dumerili*, greater amberjack.
41-8. *Seriola rivoliana*, almaco jack.
41-9. *Seriolina nigrofasciata*, blackbanded trevally.
41-10. *Trachinotus baillonii*, smallspotted dart.
41-11. *Trachurus indicus*, Arabian scad.
41-12. *Uraspis helvola*, whitetongue jack.

## PLATE 42

42-1. *Aphareus furca* (25 cm), Christmas Island, 15 m.
42-2. *Lutjanus decussatus* (40 cm), Phuket, Thailand, 3 m.
42-3. *Lutjanus bengalensis* (10 cm), Mauritius, 25 m.
42-4. *Lutjanus kasmira* (10 cm), Mauritius, 25 m.
42-5. *Lutjanus notatus* (10 cm), Mauritius, 25 m.
42-6. *Lutjanus ehrenbergii* (18 cm), Kosi Bay, South Africa, 2 m.
42-7. *Lutjanus argentimaculatus* (45 cm), Persian Gulf, 3 m.
42-8. *Lutjanus fulviflamma* (32 cm), Mahe, Seychelles, 8 m.

## PLATE 43

43-1. *Lutjanus bohar* (16 cm), Shimoni, Kenya, 10 m.
43-2. *Lutjanus fulvus* (20 cm), Watamu, Kenya, 25 m.
43-3. *Lutjanus monostigma* (38 cm), Vilingilli, Maldive Islands, 15 m.
43-4. *Lutjanus lunulatus* (35 cm), Similan Islands, Andaman Sea, 15 m.
43-5. *Lutjanus madras* (20 cm), Phuket, Thailand, 5 m.
43-6. *Lutjanus biguttatus* (25 cm), Great Barrier Reef, 12 m.
43-7. *Lutjanus gibbus* (35 cm), Vilingilli, Maldive Islands, 10 m.
43-8. *Lutjanus gibbus* (35 cm), Vilingilli, Maldive Islands, 12 m.

## PLATE 44

44-1. *Lutjanus sebae* (30 cm), Great Barrier Reef, 6 m.
44-2. *Lutjanus vitta* (15 cm), Phuket, Thailand, 5 m.
44-3. *Macolor niger* (12 cm), Christmas Island, 12 m.
44-4. *Macolor niger* (25 cm), Vilingilli, Maldive Islands, 10 m.
44-5. *Macolor niger* (38 cm), Vilingilli, Maldive Islands, 40 m.
44-6. *Symphorus nematophorus* (35 cm), Great Barrier Reef, 10 m.
44-7. *Caesio caerulaureus* (23 cm), Vilingilli, Maldive Islands, 10 m.
44-8. *Caesio xanthonotus* (25 cm), Sodwana Bay, South Africa, 12 m.

## PLATE 45

45-1. *Caesio xanthonotus* (25 cm), Great Barrier Reef, 10 m.
45-2. *Pterocaesio striatus* (18 cm), Jeddah, Red Sea, 6 m.
45-3. *Pterocaesio chrysozona* (16 cm), Phuket, Thailand, 5 m.
45-4. *Pterocaesio chrysozona* (16 cm), Christmas Island, 12 m.
45-5. *Pterocaesio tile* (20 cm), Vilingilli, Maldive Islands, 12 m.
45-6. *Pterocaesio tile* (16 cm), Mauritius, 8 m.
45-7. *Pterocaesio sp.* (20 cm), Similan Islands, Andaman Sea, 15 m.
45-8. *Pterocaesio sp.* (14 cm), Watamu, Kenya, 12 m.

## PLATE 46

46-1. *Chrysoblephus anglicus* (38 cm), Aliwal Shoal, South Africa, 15 m.
46-2. *Diplodus cervinus* (15 cm), Sodwana Bay, South Africa, 15 m.
46-3. *Diplodus sargus capensis* (10 cm), Sodwana Bay, South Africa, 2 m.
46-4. *Porcostoma dentata* (28 cm), Durban Aquarium, South Africa.
46-5. *Rhabdosargus auroventris* (12 cm), Kosi Bay, South Africa, 2 m.
46-6. *Gymnocranius griseus* (20 cm), Sodwana Bay, South Africa, 22 m.
46-7. *Monotaxis grandoculis* (10 cm), Great Barrier Reef, 5 m.
46-8. *Monotaxis grandoculus* (45 cm), Vilingilli, Maldive Islands, 12 m.

PLATE 53

53-1. The young of several jack species form symbiotic associations with jellyfish. The fishes are protected from predators among the stinging tentacles during the most vulnerable stage of their life history. This photograph was taken at the Similan Islands, Andaman Sea.

53-2 to 6. One of the most interesting symbiotic relationships involves tropical comasterid crinoids and several small fishes and invertebrates. The crinoid (5) provides a source of food or shelter for its occupants which are remarkably well camouflaged. The symbiotic animals include (2) a fish, *Lepadichthys caritus* (family Gobiesocidae), (3) a shrimp, (4) a crab, and (6) an ophiuroid - lower right. All photos taken at Christmas Island in 10 m.

53-7. *Amphiprion nigripes*, family Pomacentridae (9 cm), Vilingilli, Maldive Islands, 10 m. Perhaps the most well documented case of marine symbiosis involves anemonefishes and large tropical sea anemones.

PLATE 54

54-1. *Galeocerdo cuvieri*, family Carcharhinidae (400 cm), Great Barrier Reef, 4 m. Large fishes such as this tiger shark are usually accompanied by sharksuckers or remoras which feed on small scraps provided by the feeding activities of their host.

54-2. *Echeneis naucrates*, family Echeneidae (50 cm), Great Barrier Reef, 10 m. The remora has an unusual flattened head with the dorsal fin modified to form a sucking apparatus which is used for attachment to the host fish, turtle, or whale.

54-3. Gobiesocid species (3 cm), Recherche Archipelago, Western Australia, 15 m. This undescribed clingfish is frequently found living with sponges on reefs off southwestern Australia.

54-4. The same clingfish featured in the previous illustration is sometimes seen adhering to the surface of large fishes such as this harlequin grouper (family Serranidae). It apparently feeds on the mucous coating.

54-5. Cleaner wrasses belonging to the genus *Labroides* (family Labridae) provide a service that is vital to the wellbeing of the reef fish community. They feed on ectoparasites of other fishes that periodically visit permanent sites on the reef known as "cleaning stations." This 18 cm triggerfish, *Balistapus undulatus*, is being inspected by *Labroides dimidiatus*, Maldive Islands, 5 m.

54-6. Large fishes such as this grouper (*Plectropoma* sp.) patiently remain motionless while being worked over by cleanerfish. The cleaners frequently enter the mouth cavity and gills. Maldive Islands, 15 m.

54-7. A cleanerfish (*Labroides dimidiatus*) emerges from the mouth cavity of a large sweetlips, *Plectorhinchus pictus*. Great Barrier Reef, 3 m.

54-8. Several other fishes, most notably the young of various wrasses, butterflyfishes, and angelfishes, sometimes fill the role of ectoparasite cleaners. This butterflyfish, *Heniochus intermedius*, is being cleaned by a young wrasse, *Bodianus anthioides*. Gulf of Aqaba, Red Sea, 8 m.

## PLATE 55

55-1 & 2. Shrimps that belong to the genus *Periclimenes* also provide cleaning service. They are often seen crawling on the surface of large moray eels. This small shrimp is delicately inspecting a juvenile cardinalfish, *Apogon aureus*. Similan Islands, Andaman Sea, 3 m.

55-3. *Pseudolabrus biserialis*, family Labridae (14 cm), Recherche Archipelago, Western Australia, 10 m. Reef fishes such as this small wrasse are sometimes parasitized by isopods, a specialized crustacean that attaches to the surface of the fish during an early stage of its life history. It receives nourishment by feeding on the tissues of its host. Although the presence of one or more amphipods probably decreases the fish's life span, they nevertheless manage to cope with the infestation for lengthy periods and behave normally.

55-4. *Amphiprion akallopisos*, family Pomacentridae (10 cm), Mahe, Seychelles, 5 m. This anemonefish is parasitized by the cymothoid isopod *Renocilia heterozota*.

55-5. A pair of *Cryptocentrus* gobies with their commensal alpheid shrimp. The shrimp continually cleans and expands the sandy burrow which provides shelter for the fish.

## PLATE 56

56-1. *Chaetodon aureofasciatus* (10 cm), Great Barrier Reef, 3 m.

56-2. *Chaetodon blackburni* (8 cm), Mauritius, 10 m.

56-3. *Chaetodon ulietensis* (10 cm), Great Barrier Reef, 5 m.

56-4. *Chaetodon falcula* (15 cm), Vilingilli, Maldive Islands, 5 m.

56-5. *Chaetodon fasciatus* (16 cm), Gulf of Aqaba, Red Sea, 10 m.

56-6. *Chaetodon lunula* (30 cm), Houtman Abrolhos, Western Australia, 6 m.

56-7. *Chaetodon kleinii* (14 cm), Vilingilli, Maldive Islands, 15 m.

56-8. *Chaetodon kleinii* (16 cm), Christmas Island, 12 m.

## PLATE 57

57-1. *Chaetodon assarius* (10 cm), Houtman Abrolhos, Western Australia, 6 m.

57-2. *Chaetodon dolosus* (15 cm), Sodwana Bay, South Africa, 30 m.

57-3. *Chaetodon melapterus* (10 cm), Muscat, Oman, 4 m.

57-4. *Chaetodon austriacus* (12 cm), Gulf of Aqaba, Red Sea, 6 m.

57-5. *Chaetodon bennetti* (15 cm), Vilingilli, Maldive Islands, 15 m.

57-6. *Chaetodon trifasciatus* (10 cm), Christmas Island, 10 m.

57-7. *Chaetodon citrinellus* (10 cm), Great Barrier Reef, 6 m.

57-8. *Chaetodon collare* (15 cm), Vilingilli, Maldive Islands, 5 m.

## PLATE 58

58-1. *Chaetodon triangulum* (10 cm), Vilingilli, Maldive Islands, 10 m.

58-2. *Chaetodon larvatus* (12 cm), Jeddah, Red Sea, 3 m.

58-3. *Chaetodon leucopleura* (12 cm), Shimoni, Kenya, 12 m.

58-4. *Chaetodon trifascialis* (7 cm), Malindi, Kenya, 15 m.

58-5. *Chaetodon paucifasciatus* (12 cm), Gulf of Aqaba, Red Sea, 10 m.

58-6. *Chaetodon madagascariensis* (15 cm), Vilingilli, Maldive Islands, 15 m.

58-7. *Chaetodon melannotus* (12 cm), Vilingilli, Maldive Islands, 8 m.

58-8. *Chaetodon ocellicaudus* (10 cm), Cebu, Philippines, 8 m. Note the strong similarity to the closely related *C. melannotus* which lacks the round spot at the middle of the caudal fin base.

## PLATE 59

59-1. *Chaetodon meyeri* (18 cm), Christmas Island, 15 m.

59-2. *Chaetodon ornatissimus* (18 cm), Christmas Island, 12 m.

59-3. *Chaetodon nigropunctatus* (10 cm), Muscat, Oman, 6 m.

59-4. *Chaetodon octofasciatus* (8 cm), Phuket, Thailand, 5 m.

59-5. *Chaetodon lineolatus* (25 cm), Great Barrier Reef, 10 m.

59-6. *Chaetodon oxycephalus* (15 cm), Vilingilli, Maldive Islands, 8 m.

59-7. *Chaetodon plebeius* (8 cm), Similan Islands, Andaman Sea, 10 m.

59-8. *Chaetodon plebeius* (8 cm), Christmas Island, 6 m.

## PLATE 60

60-1. *Chaetodon unimaculatus* (12 cm), Christmas Island, 10 m.

60-2. *Chaetodon unimaculatus* (8 cm), Mauritius, 12 m.

60-3. *Chaetodon mitratus* (8 cm), Christmas Island, 40 m.

60-4. *Chaetodon marleyi* (13 cm), Sodwana Bay, South Africa, 2 m.

60-5. *Chaetodon xanthocephalus* (15 cm), Mahe, Seychelles, 10 m.

60-6. *Chaetodon ephippium* (20 cm), Great Barrier Reef, 10 m.

60-7. *Chaetodon auriga* (20 cm), Vilingilli, Maldive Islands, 10 m.

60-8. *Chaetodon rafflesi* (14 cm), Ishigaki, Japan, 8 m.

## PLATE 61

61-1. *Chaetodon guttatissimus* (12 cm), Christmas Island, 6 m.

61-2. *Chaetodon punctatofasciatus* (10 cm), Great Barrier Reef, 15 m.

61-3. *Chaetodon semilarvatus* (18 cm), Gulf of Aqaba, Red Sea, 10 m.

61-4. *Chaetodon semeion* (15 cm), Rabaul, New Britain, 15 m.

61-5. *Chaetodon speculum* (15 cm), Great Barrier Reef, 10 m.

61-6. *Chaetodon zanzibariensis* (15 cm), Mahe, Seychelles, 10 m.

61-7. *Chaetodon decussatus* (18 cm), Trincomalee, Sri Lanka, 7 m.

61-8. *Chaetodon vagabundus* (10 cm), Great Barrier Reef, 5 m.

## PLATE 62

62-1. *Forcipiger longirostris* (12 cm), Christmas Island, 12 m.

62-2. *Forcipiger longirostris* (12 cm), Christmas Island, 12 m.

62-3. *Forcipiger longirostris* (12 cm), Christmas Island, 12 m.

62-4. *Forcipiger flavissimus* (8 cm), Rabaul, New Britain, 3 m.

62-5. *Hemitaurichthys polylepis* (12 cm), Great Barrier Reef, 20 m.

62-6. *Hemitaurichthys zoster* (16 cm), Similan Islands, Andaman Sea, 20 m.

62-7. *Heniochus acuminatus* (24 cm), Houtman Abrolhos, Western Australia, 20 m.

62-8. *Heniochus monoceros* (22 cm), Vilingilli, Maldive Islands, 15 m.

## PLATE 63

63-1. *Heniochus pleurotaenia* (18 cm), Vilingilli, Maldive Islands, 8 m.

63-2. *Heniochus diphreutes* (18 cm), Vilingilli, Maldive Islands, 10 m.

63-3. *Chelmon marginalis* (12 cm), Great Barrier Reef, 8 m.

63-4. *Parachaetodon ocellatus* (10 cm), Houtman Abrolhos, Western Australia, 2 m.

63-5. *Chelmonops truncatus* (20 cm), Recherche Archipelago, Western Australia, 10 m.

63-6. *Coradion chrysozonus* (6 cm), North West Cape, Western Australia, 3 m.

## PLATE 64

64-1. *Tilodon sexfasciatum* (8 cm), Recherche Archipelago, Western Australia, 6 m.

64-2. *Tilodon sexfasciatum* (18 cm), Geographe Bay, Western Australia, 10 m.

64-3. *Kyphosus cornelii* (35 cm), Houtman Abrolhos, Western Australia, 4 m.

64-4. *Kyphosus sydneyanus* (30 cm), Houtman Abrolhos, Western Australia, 10 m.

64-5. *Girella zebra* (30 cm), Recherche Archipelago, Western Australia, 15 m.

64-6. *Microcanthus strigatus* (12 cm), Houtman Abrolhos, Western Australia, 3 m.

64-7. *Neatypus obliquus* (18 cm), Recherche Archipelago, Western Australia, 10 m.

64-8. *Scorpis georgianus* (23 cm), Houtman Abrolhos, Western Australia, 10 m.

## PLATE 65

65-1. *Enoplosus armatus* (24 cm), Recherche Archipelago, Western Australia, 8 m.

65-2. *Pentaceropsis recurvirostris* (38 cm), Geographe Bay, Western Australia, 10 m.

65-3. *Drepane punctata* (16 cm), Durban Aquarium, South Africa.

65-4. *Platax tiere* (33 cm), Durban Aquarium, South Africa.

65-5. *Platax tiere* (6 cm), Mombasa, Kenya, 4 m.

65-6. *Platax tiere* (20 cm), Similan Islands, Andaman Sea, 10 m.

## PLATE 66
66-1. *Apolemichthys trimaculatus* (13 cm), Vilingilli, Maldive Islands, 22 m.
66-2. *Apolemichthys xanthurus* (15 cm), Hikkaduwa, Sri Lanka, 8 m.
66-3. *Centropyge acanthops* (5 cm), Shimoni, Kenya, 15 m.
66-4. *Centropyge bicolor* (10 cm), Great Barrier Reef, 10 m.
66-5. *Centropyge bispinosus* (8 cm), Great Barrier Reef, 6 m.
66-6. *Centropyge eibli* (10 cm), Christmas Island, 15 m.
66-7. *Centropyge flavipectoralis* (10 cm), Trincomalee, Sri Lanka, 12 m.
66-8. *Centropyge multispinis* (12 cm), Similan Islands, Andaman Sea, 12 m.

## PLATE 67
67-1. *Centropyge flavissimus* (6 cm), Christmas Island, 12 m.
67-2. *Centropyge flavissimus* (14 cm), Christmas Island, 5 m.
67-3. *Centropyge multifasciatus* (10 cm), Rabaul, New Britain, 20 m.
67-4. *Centropyge joculator* (6 cm), Christmas Island, 20 m.
67-5. *Centropyge tibicen* (7 cm), Christmas Island, 15 m.
67-6. *Centropyge vroliki* (10 cm), Great Barrier Reef, 5 m.
67-7. *Genicanthus caudovittatus*, male (20 cm), Gulf of Aqaba, Red Sea, 30 m.
67-8. *Genicanthus caudovittatus*, female (15 cm), Gulf of Aqaba, Red Sea, 25 m.

## PLATE 68
68-1. *Pomacanthus striatus* (35 cm), Sodwana Bay, South Africa, 15 m.
68-2. *Pomacanthus semicirculatus* (22 cm), Malindi, Kenya, 7 m.
68-3. *Pomacanthus chrysurus* (24 cm), Malindi, Kenya, 7 m.
68-4. *Euxiphipops sexstriatus* (32 cm), Great Barrier Reef, 8 m.
68-5. *Euxiphipops navarchus* (20 cm), Rabaul, New Britain, 25 m.
68-6. *Euxiphipops xanthometapon* (42 cm), Vilingilli, Maldive Islands, 15 m.
68-7. *Pygoplites diacanthus* (20 cm), Vilingilli, Maldive Islands, 10 m.
68-8. *Arusetta asfur* (25 cm), Jeddah, Red Sea, 6 m.

## PLATE 69
69-1. *Pomacanthus annularis* (8 cm), Phuket, Thailand, 4 m.
69-2. *Pomacanthus annularis* (25 cm), Colombo, Sri Lanka, 5 m.
69-3. *Pomacanthus imperator* (10 cm), Similan Islands, Andaman Sea, 10 m.
69-4. *Pomacanthus imperator* (30 cm), Vilingilli, Maldive Islands, 10 m.
69-5. *Pomacanthus maculosus* (40 cm), Mombasa, Kenya, 8 m.

## PLATE 70
70-1. *Chaetodon trifascialis* (12 cm), Great Barrier Reef, 5 m.
70-2. *Anomalops katoptron* (6 cm), Cebu, Philippines, 22 m.
70-3. Mucous cocoon of *Scarus* sp. (12 cm), Great Barrier Reef, 4 m.
70-4. Mucous cocoon of *Scarus psittacus*, male (35 cm), Great Barrier Reef, 4 m.
70-5. *Zanclus cornutus* (18 cm), Great Barrier Reef, 10 m.
70-6. *Gymnothorax meleagris* (75 cm), Christmas Island, 10 m.
70-7. *Priacanthus hamrur* (30 cm), Vilingilli, Maldive Islands, 10 m.
70-8. *Myripristis axillaris* (20 cm), Christmas Island, 10 m.

## PLATE 71
71-1. *Abudefduf bengalensis* (15 cm), Houtman Abrolhos, Western Australia, 4 m.
71-2. *Abudefduf margariteus* (6 cm), Mauritius, 3 m.
71-3. *Abudefduf notatus* (15 cm), Sodwana Bay, South Africa, 1 m.
71-4. *Abudefduf sexfasciatus* (15 cm), Mauritius, 6 m.
71-5. *Abudefduf sparoides* (12 cm), Malindi, Kenya, 10 m.
71-6. *Amblyglyphidodon flavilatus* (10 cm), Gulf of Aqaba, Red Sea, 20 m.
71-7. *Amblyglyphidodon leucogaster* (13 cm), Vilingilli, Maldive Islands, 4 m.
71-8. *Lepidozygus tapeinosoma* (10 cm), Vilingilli, Maldive Islands, 6 m.

## PLATE 72

72-1. *Amphiprion akallopisos* (10 cm), Phuket, Thailand, 6 m.
72-2. *Amphiprion akallopisos* (9 cm), Mahe, Seychelles, 8 m.
72-3. *Amphiprion allardi* (12 cm), Shimoni, Kenya, 5 m.
72-4. *Amphiprion clarkii* (12 cm), Vilingilli, Maldive Islands, 10 m.
72-5. *Amphiprion chrysogaster* (12 cm), Mauritius, 8 m.
72-6. *Amphiprion chrysogaster* (5 cm), Mauritius, 4 m.
72-7. *Amphiprion ephippium* (8 cm), Phuket, Thailand, 4 m.
72-8. *Amphiprion fuscocaudatus* (10 cm), Mahe, Seychelles, 10 m.

## PLATE 73

73-1. *Amphiprion nigripes* (2 cm), Trincomalee, Sri Lanka, 20 m.
73-2. *Amphiprion nigripes* (7 cm), Vilingilli, Maldive Islands, 10 m.
73-3. *Amphiprion ocellaris* (6 cm), Phuket, Thailand, 4 m.
73-4. *Amphiprion sebae* (10 cm), Trincomalee, Sri Lanka, 12 m.
73-5. *Dascyllus carneus* (5 cm), Phuket, Thailand, 3 m.
73-6. *Dascyllus aruanus* (4 cm), Mauritius, 5 m.
73-7. *Dascyllus trimaculatus* (3 cm), Mauritius, 4 m.
73-8. *Parma bicolor* (20 cm), Recherche Archipelago, Western Australia, 12 m.

## PLATE 74

74-1. *Chromis atripectoralis* (10 cm), Christmas Island, 12 m.
74-2. *Chromis axillaris* (12 cm), Gulf of Aqaba, Red Sea, 35 m.
74-3. *Chromis virida* (male, guarding eggs) (6 cm), Jeddah, Red Sea, 4 m.
74-4. *Chromis dimidiata* (6 cm), Gulf of Aqaba, Red Sea, 10 m.
74-5. *Chromis elerae* (6 cm), Vilingilli, Maldive Islands, 25 m.
74-6. *Chromis klunzingeri* (10 cm), Recherche Archipelago, Western Australia, 15 m.
74-7. *Chromis nigrura* (5 cm), Christmas Island, 3 m.
74-8. *Chromis opercularis* (5 cm), Mahe, Seychelles, 8 m.

## PLATE 75

75-1. *Chrysiptera biocellata* (10 cm), Vilingilli, Maldive Islands, 1 m.
75-2. *Chrysiptera glauca* (3 cm), Mauritius, 1 m.
75-3. *Chrysiptera unimaculata* (8 cm), Christmas Island, 1 m.
75-4. *Chrysiptera unimaculata* (3 cm), Mauritius, 2 m.
75-5. *Chrysiptera rollandi* (6 cm), Phuket, Thailand, 10 m.
75-6. *Neopomacentrus miryae* (5 cm), Gulf of Aqaba, Red Sea, 20 m.
75-7. *Plectroglyphidodon leucozonus* (8 cm), Mauritius, 1 m.
75-8. *Plectroglyphidodon phoenixensis* (5 cm), Christmas Island, 1 m.

## PLATE 76

76-1. *Pomacentrus philippinus* (8 cm), Phuket, Thailand, 4 m.
76-2. *Pomacentrus trichourus* (8 cm), Sodwana Bay, South Africa, 25 m.
76-3. *Pomacentrus caeruleus* (7 cm), Mahe, Seychelles, 10 m.
76-4. *Pomacentrus alleni* (6 cm), Phuket, Thailand, 5 m.
76-5. *Pomacentrus coelestis* (6 cm), Christmas Island, 15 m.

## PLATE 77

77-1. *Pomacentrus chrysurus* (8 cm), Phuket, Thailand, 5 m.
77-2. *Pomacentrus pavo* (8 cm), Phuket, Thailand, 5 m.
77-3. *Pomacentrus pikei* (12 cm), Mauritius, 3 m.
77-4. *Pomacentrus trilineatus* (8 cm), Jeddah, Red Sea, 3 m.
77-5. *Pomacentrus* sp. (10 cm), Shimoni, Kenya, 4 m.
77-6. *Stegastes fasciolatus* (12 cm), Vilingilli, Maldive Islands, 1 m.
77-7. *Stegastes insularis* (9 cm), Christmas Island, 4 m.
77-8. *Stegastes* sp. (8 cm), Mauritius, 5 m.

## PLATE 78

78-1. *Cirrhitichthys oxycephalus* (8 cm), Christmas Island, 8 m.

78-2. *Cirrhitichthys bleekeri* (7 cm), Colombo, Sri Lanka, 4 m.

78-3. *Cirrhitichthys aprinus* (7 cm), Batangas, Philippines, 10 m.

78-4. *Cirrhitichthys guichenoti* (8 cm), Mauritius, 25 m.

78-5. *Cirrhitichthys oxycephalus* (8 cm), Watamu, Kenya, 10 m.

## PLATE 79

79-1. *Cirrhitops fasciatus* (8 cm), Mauritius, 25 m.

79-2. *Cyprinocirrhites polyactis* (8 cm), Mauritius, 25 m.

79-3. *Paracirrhites arcuatus* (13 cm), Christmas Island, 10 m.

79-4. *Paracirrhites forsteri* (14 cm), Christmas Island, 10 m.

79-5. *Paracirrhites hemistictus* (19 cm), Christmas Island, 4 m.

79-6. *Paracirrhites hemistictus* (*polystictus* phase) (20 cm), Great Barrier Reef, 8 m.

79-7. *Cirrhitus pinnulatus* (16 cm), Christmas Island, 8 m.

79-8. *Oxycirrhitus typus* (8 cm), Vilingilli, Maldive Islands, 30 m.

## PLATE 80

80-1. *Cheilodactylus nigripes* (24 cm), Recherche Archipelago, Western Australia, 10 m.

80-2. *Cheilodactylus rubrolabiatus* (50 cm), Houtman Abrolhos, Western Australia, 10 m.

80-3. *Dactylosargus* sp. (40 cm), Recherche Archipelago, Western Australia, 10 m.

80-4. *Dactylophora nigricans* (50 cm), Recherche Archipelago, Western Australia, 12 m.

80-5. *Chirodactylus brachydactylus* (30 cm), Aliwal Shoal, South Africa, 20 m.

80-6. *Chirodactylus brachydactylus* (38 cm), Aliwal Shoal, South Africa, 10 m.

80-7. *Monodactylus argenteus* (14 cm), Kosi Bay, South Africa, 3 m.

80-8. *Monodactylus falciformes* (15 cm), Kosi Bay, South Africa, 2 m.

## PLATE 81

81-1. *Acanthurus triostegus* (20 cm), Christmas Island, 5 m. Surgeonfishes represent one of the primary groups of algal feeding fishes on Indo-Pacific reefs.

81-2. *Scarus prasiognathus*, family Scaridae (50 cm), Vilingilli, Maldive Islands, 3 m. Group feeding is also employed by the parrotfishes. Scarids feed on filamentous algae which closely adheres to the surface of the reef. While feeding they ingest large amounts of calcareous material which is voided with the feces and contributes significantly to the overall bottom sediment. This unusual aggregation is stratified with males on top and somber colored females below.

81-3. *Acanthurus leucosternon*, family Acanthuridae (24 cm), Vilingilli, Maldive Islands, 6 m. Group feeding is an effective strategy which has evolved in the surgeonfishes. It enables them to enter the territories of aggressive species such as damselfish without being harassed and driven away, which happens when individuals intrude.

81-4. *Arothron hispidus*, family Tetraodontidae (25 cm), Houtman Abrolhos, Western Australia, 10 m. This pufferfish has just taken a bite from the tip of a branch of *Acropora* coral.

81-5. *Choerodon rubescens*, family Labridae (35 cm), Houtman Abrolhos, Western Australia, 5 m. *Choerodon* wrasses possess powerful dentition which they use to lift rocks off the bottom in search of molluscs. This individual has found a turban shell.

81-6. *Taenioconger haasi*, Congridae (60 cm), Great Barrier Reef, 10 m. Garden eels live in sand burrows in areas where currents are swift. They feed on minute planktonic animals.

81-7. *Anthias evansi* (yellow back) and *A. squamipinnis*, family Serranidae (10 cm), Vilingilli, Maldive Islands, 10 m. Unlike most serranids, which are predators of small fishes, the fairy basslets form midwater aggregations that feed on plankton.

PLATE 82

82-1 to 4. Like a swarm of vicious piranhas, black triggerfish, *Melichthys indicus*, quickly reduce a dead lionfish to shreds. The authors conducted this experiment at Christmas Island to determine if reef predators would feed on the venomous-spined lionfish.

82-5. *Synodus* sp. (18 cm), Gulf of Aqaba, Red Sea, 5 m. This lizardfish has captured a juvenile *Lethrinus* with a lightening swift strike.

82-6. *Valenciennea strigata* (15 cm), Malindi, Kenya, 6 m. Many gobies feed on benthic detritus which is scooped into the mouth and sieved through the gills. The surplus sand passes out through the gill openings.

82-7. *Bothus mancus* (18 cm), Christmas Island, 12 m.

82-8. *Bothus mancus* (18 cm), Christmas Island, 12 m.

PLATE 83

83-1. *Anampses caeruleopunctatus* (15 cm), Similan Islands, Andaman Sea, 10 m.

83-2. *Anampses lennardi* (18 cm), Dampier Archipelago, Western Australia, 3 m.

83-3. *Anampses melanurus lineatus* (15 cm), Similan Islands, Andaman Sea, 25 m.

83-4. *Anampses twisti* (12 cm), Watamu, Kenya, 8 m.

83-5. *Bodianus opercularis* (12 cm), Christmas Island, 50 m.

83-6. *Bodianus bimaculatus* (8 cm), Mauritius (aquarium photo).

83-7. *Bodianus axillaris* (8 cm), Shimoni, Kenya, 8 m.

83-8. *Bodianus axillaris* (17 cm), Vilingilli, Maldive Islands, 5 m.

PLATE 84

84-1. *Bodianus bilunulatus* (4 cm), Sodwana Bay, South Africa, 25 m.

84-2. *Bodianus bilunulatus* (24 cm), Mauritius, 28 m.

84-3. *Bodianus anthioides* (10 cm), Watamu, Kenya, 15 m.

84-4. *Bodianus diana* (18 cm), Watamu, Kenya, 12 m.

84-5. *Bodianus frenchi* (30 cm), Recherche Archipelago, Western Australia, 12 m.

84-6. *Bodianus macrurus* (28 cm), Mauritius, 8 m.

84-7. *Choerodon rubescens* (24 cm), Houtman Abrolhos, Western Australia, 15 m.

84-8. *Achoerodus gouldii* (70 cm), Recherche Archipelago, Western Australia, 18 m.

PLATE 85

85-1. *Cheilinus bimaculatus*, female (10 cm), Watamu, Kenya, 15 m.

85-2. *Cheilinus bimaculatus*, male (10 cm), Mauritius, 15 m.

85-3. *Cheilinus diagrammus* (10 cm), Vilingilli, Maldive Islands, 6 m.

85-4. *Cheilinus diagrammus* (25 cm), Great Barrier Reef, 12 m. The white band at the base of the tail can be switched on or off instantaneously.

85-5. *Cheilinus diagrammus* (15 cm), Mahe, Seychelles, 6 m.

85-6. *Cheilinus fasciatus* (24 cm), Mahe, Seychelles, 8 m.

85-7. *Cheilinus lunulatus* (70 cm), Gulf of Aqaba, Red Sea, 12 m.

85-8. *Cheilinus trilobatus* (30 cm), Mahe, Seychelles, 10 m.

PLATE 86

86-1. *Cheilinus undulatus* (100 cm), Vilingilli, Maldive Islands, 22 m.

86-2. *Cheilinus* sp. (16 cm), Gulf of Aqaba, Red Sea, 10 m.

86-3. *Cheilinus chlorurus* (20 cm), Mahe, Seychelles, 15 m.

86-4. *Cirrhilabrus* sp. (10 cm), Mauritius (aquarium photo).

86-5. *Cirrhilabrus cyanopleura*, female (8 cm), Similan Islands, Andaman Sea, 15 m.

86-6. *Cirrhilabrus cyanopleura*, male (12 cm), Similan Islands, Andaman Sea, 15 m.

86-7. *Cirrhilabrus exquisita*, male (10 cm), Vilingilli, Maldive Islands, 8 m.

86-8. *Cirrhilabrus exquisita*, female (6 cm), Vilingilli, Maldive Islands, 8 m.

PLATE 87

87-1. *Conniella apterygia*, male (8 cm), Rowley Shoals (aquarium photo).

87-2. *Coris caudimacula* (18 cm), Malindi, Kenya, 5 m.

87-3. *Coris auricularis*, male (30 cm), Houtman Abrolhos, Western Australia, 10 m.

87-4. *Coris auricularis*, male juvenile (5 cm), Houtman Abrolhos, Western Australia, 5 m.

87-5. *Coris aygula* (10 cm), Mombasa, Kenya, 7 m.

87-6. *Coris aygula* (25 cm), Christmas Island, 10 m.

87-7. *Coris variegata* (13 cm), Vilingilli, Maldive Islands, 34 m.

87-8. *Coris variegata* (15 cm), Gulf of Aqaba, Red Sea, 15 m.

**Captions to Plates 88–144 begin on page 209**

1
2
3
4
5
6

**PLATE #1**

65

66

**PLATE #2**

**PLATE #3**

1 ►

2 ►

3 ►

4 ►

5 ►

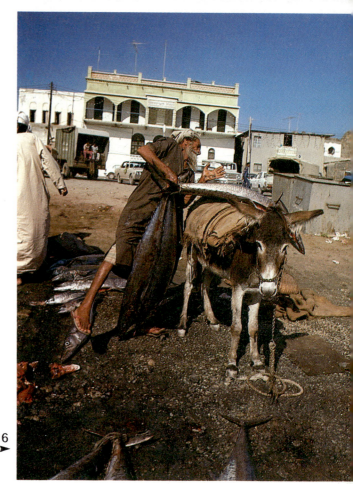

6 ►

**PLATE #4**

1 ◄

2 ◄

3 ◄

4 ▼

PLATE #5                    69

1

2

3

4

5

6

**PLATE #6**

**PLATE #7**

71

**PLATE #8**

1

2

3

4

5

6

7

8

9

10

11a

11b

12    13    14

**PLATE #9**

**PLATE #10**

**PLATE #11**

75

**PLATE #12**

**PLATE #13**

1
2
3
4
5
6
7

PLATE #14

**PLATE #15**

79

**PLATE #16**

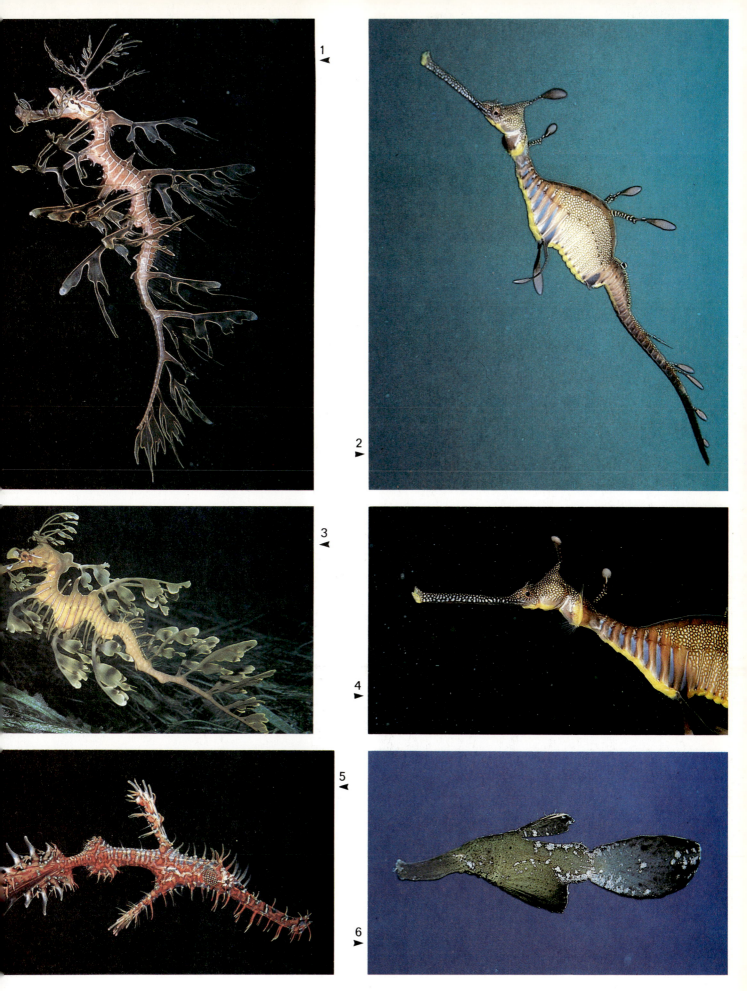

PLATE #17                    81

**PLATE #18**

**1**

**2**

**3**

**4**

**5**

**PLATE #19**

83

84 **PLATE #20**

**PLATE #21**

85

1
◄

2
►

3
◄

4
►

5
◄

6
►

7
◄

8
►

**PLATE #22**

**PLATE #23**                                                                                          87

1 ▲
2 ▶
3 ▶
4 ▶
5 ▶

**PLATE #24**

**PLATE #25** 89

PLATE #27                                                                          91

**PLATE #28**

PLATE #29

93

94                                    **PLATE #30**

PLATE #31

95

PLATE #33                                                      97

**PLATE #34**

**PLATE #35**

99

PLATE #36

**PLATE #37**

101

**PLATE #38**

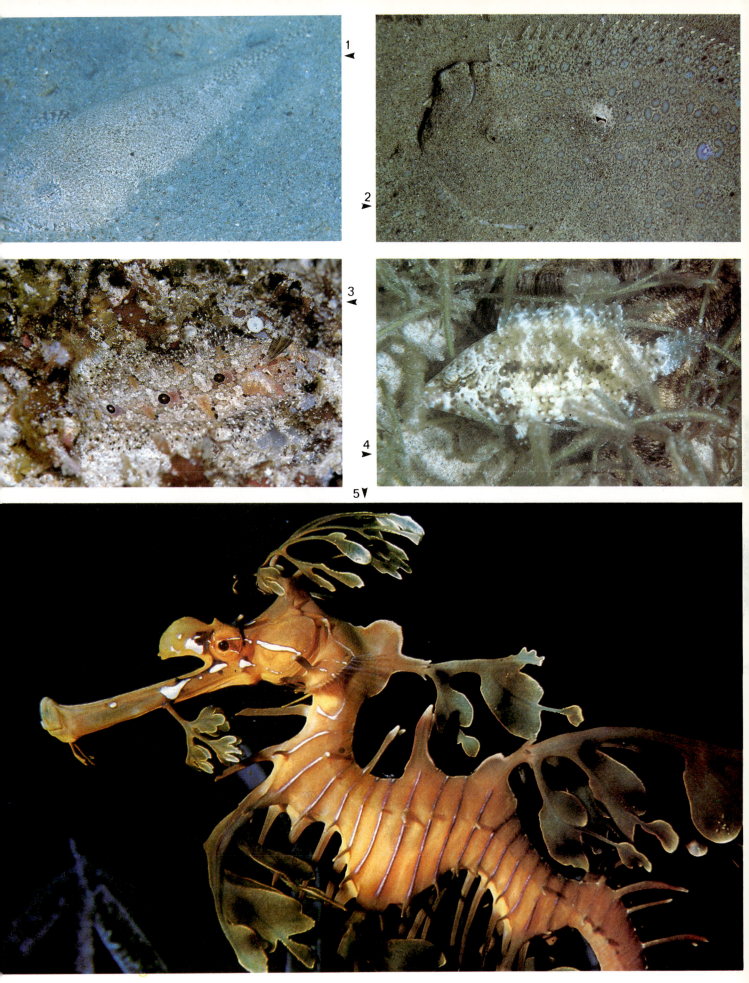

**PLATE #39**

103

**PLATE #40**

**PLATE #42**

PLATE # 43

107

**PLATE #44**

PLATE #45

109

PLATE #47

**PLATE #48**

PLATE #49                                                                                                113

1
2
3
4
5
6
7
8

PLATE #50

**PLATE #51**

115

1

2

3

4

5

6

7

116                                                    PLATE #52

PLATE #53                                                117

**PLATE #54**

1 ►
2 ►
3 ►
4 ►
5 ▼

**PLATE #55**

119

120

PLATE #56

PLATE #57                                                        121

PLATE #58

PLATE #59

123

1
2
3
4
5
6
7
8

PLATE #60

1

2

3

4

5

6

7

8

PLATE #61                    125

126

**PLATE #62**

PLATE #63

127

**PLATE #64**

**PLATE #65**

1

2

3

4

5

6

7

8

130                                   PLATE #66

**PLATE #67**

131

132

PLATE #68

PLATE #69

133

**PLATE #70**

PLATE #71

135

1 ◄
2 ►
3 ◄
4 ►
5 ◄
6 ►
7 ◄
8 ►

136

**PLATE #72**

**PLATE #73**

137

138

**PLATE #74**

**PLATE #75**

139

PLATE #76

PLATE #77

141

1 ▲

2 ◄

3 ►

4 ◄

5 ►

**PLATE #78**

PLATE #79                                          143

**PLATE #80**

PLATE #81

**PLATE #82**

**PLATE #83**

PLATE #84

PLATE #85

**PLATE #86**

PLATE #87                    151

**PLATE #88**

1▲          2▼

**PLATE #89**

1
2
3
4
5
6
7
8

**PLATE #90**

1▲        2▼

PLATE #91

**PLATE #92**

PLATE #93

157

**PLATE #94**

PLATE #95

159

**PLATE #96**

**PLATE #97**

161

1

2

3

4

5

6

7

8

PLATE #98

**PLATE #99**

163

1

2

3

4

5

6

7

8

164 PLATE #100

1
2
3
4
5

PLATE #101                    165

**PLATE #102**

PLATE #103

167

**PLATE #104**

PLATE #105

169

**PLATE #106**

PLATE #107

171

**PLATE #108**

PLATE #109

173

PLATE #110

**PLATE #111** 175

1▲    2▼

176                                    **PLATE #112**

PLATE #113

177

**PLATE #114**

PLATE #115

179

PLATE #116

PLATE #117

181

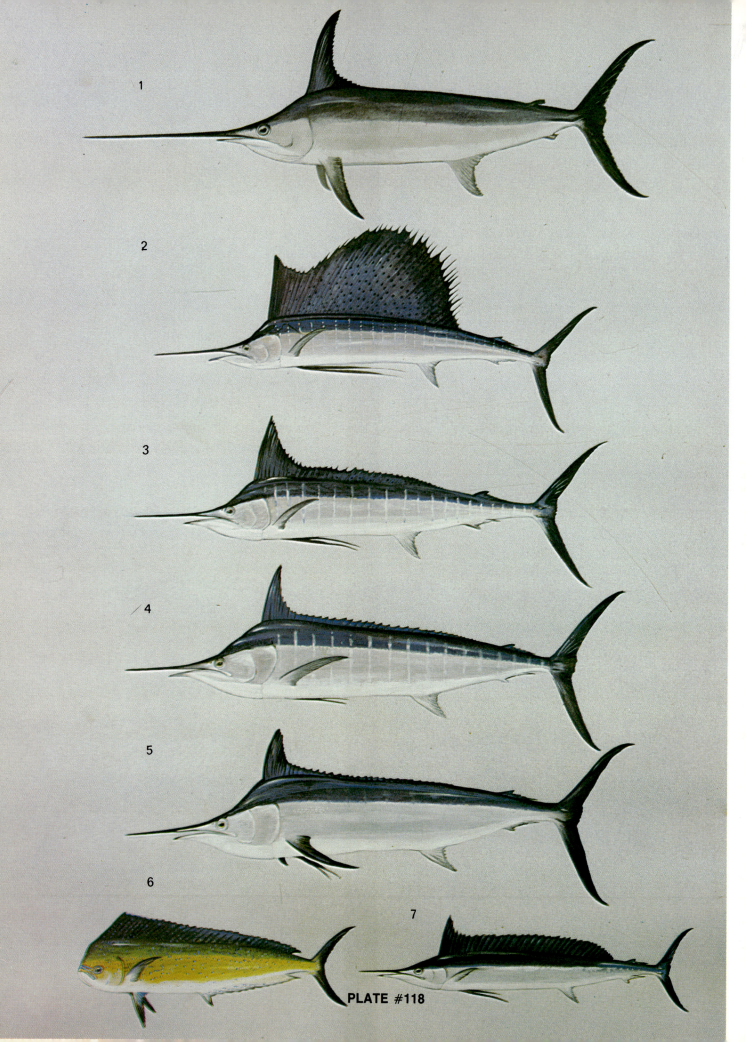

1

2

3

4

5

6

7

**PLATE #118**

**PLATE #119**

183

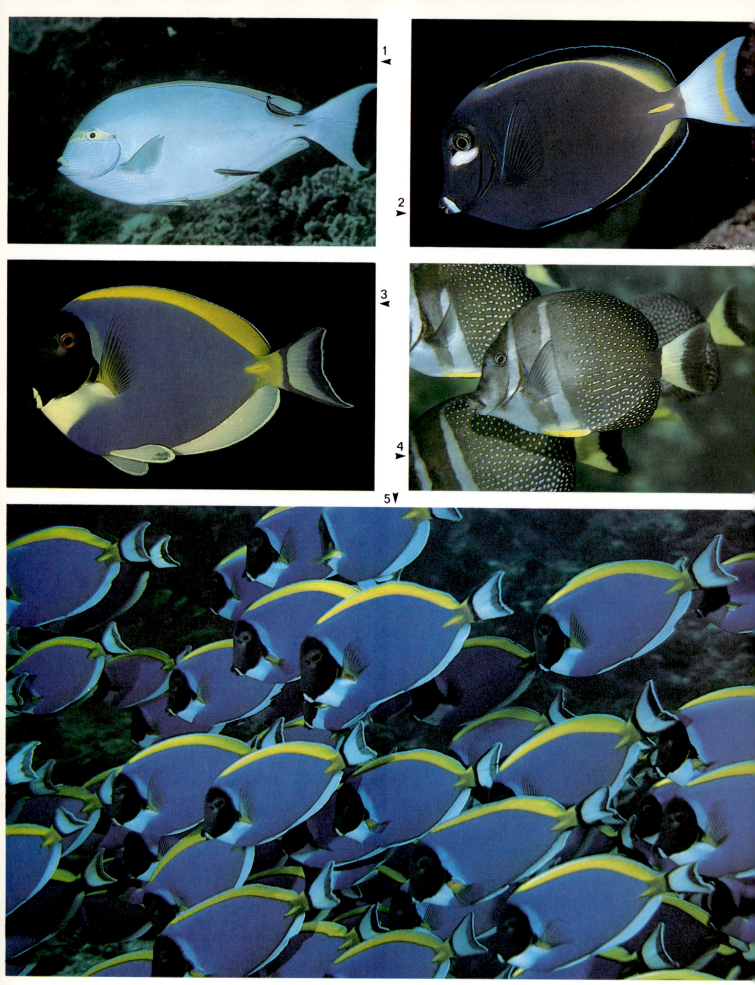

PLATE #121

185

**PLATE #122**

PLATE #123

187

**PLATE #124**

1▲ 2▼

PLATE #125

189

PLATE #127

191

1

2

3

4

5

6

7

192

**PLATE #128**

PLATE #129                                                                                        193

PLATE #131

196

**PLATE #132**

PLATE #133

197

198

**PLATE #134**

PLATE #135

199

PLATE #136

PLATE #137

201

202 PLATE #138

PLATE #139

203

PLATE #140

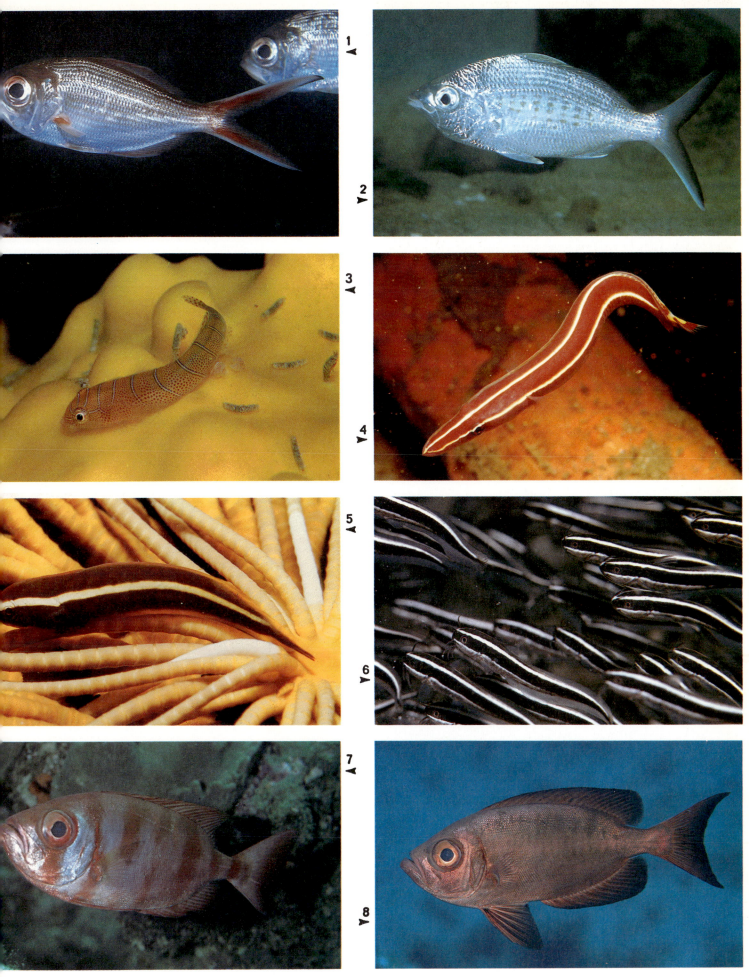

PLATE #141                                                                                                    205

1▲        2▼

**PLATE #143**

208

**PLATE #144**

# Captions to Plates 88–144

## PLATE 88

88-1. *Coris gaimardi* (30 cm), Christmas Island, 8 m.

88-2. *Coris gaimardi*, juvenile (7 cm), Great Barrier Reef, 6 m.

88-3. *Coris formosa*, female (25 cm), Hikkaduwa, Sri Lanka, 4 m.

88-4. *Coris formosa* (8 cm), Hikkaduwa, Sri Lanka, 4 m.

88-5. *Coris formosa* male (35 cm), Vilingilli, Maldive Islands, 3 m.

88-6. *Epibulus insidiator* (30 cm), Mahe, Seychelles, 12 m.

88-7. *Diproctacanthus xanthurus* (8 cm), Rabaul, New Britain, 2 m.

88-8. *Gomphosus coeruleus* (15 cm), Vilingilli, Maldive Islands, 8 m.

## PLATE 89

89-1. Senator wrasse, *Pictilabrus laticlavius*, about 8 cm TL, Geographe Bay, Western Australia, 10 m.

89-2. Slender wrasse, *Eupetrichthys angustipes*, about 12 cm TL, Esperance, Western Australia, 8 m.

## PLATE 90

90-1. *Halichoeres biocellatus* (18 cm), Christmas Island, 10 m.

90-2. *Halichoeres chrysus* (9 cm), Christmas Island, 15 m.

90-3. *Halichoeres leucoxanthus* (9 cm), Vilingilli, Maldive Islands, 12 m.

90-4. *Halichoeres nebulosus*, (10 cm), Mauritius, 1 m.

90-5. *Halichoeres marginatus*, male (15 cm), Vilingilli, Maldive Islands, 10 m.

90-6. *Halichoeres marginatus*, female (12 cm), Mauritius, 10 m.

90-7. *Halichoeres scapularis*, female (18 cm), Vilingilli, Maldive Islands, 2 m.

90-8. *Halichoeres scapularis*, male (22 cm), Kosi Bay, South Africa, 3 m.

## PLATE 91

91-1. Elongate wrasse, *Pseudojuloides elongatus*, male, about 14 cm TL, North West Cape, Western Australia, 5 m.

91-2. Brownfield's wrasse, *Halichoeres brownfieldi*, male 12 cm TL, Geographe Bay, Western Australia, 4 m.

## PLATE 92

92-1. *Halichoeres pelicieri*, female (8 cm), Mauritius (aquarium photo).

92-2. *Halichoeres iridis*, female (14 cm), Shimoni, Kenya, 25 m.

92-3. *Halichoeres malasmopomus* (10 cm), Christmas Island, 15 m.

92-4. *Halichoeres hovenii*, male (16 cm), Vilingilli, Maldive Islands, 8 m.

92-5. *Halichoeres cosmetus*, female (6 cm), Vilingilli, Maldive Islands, 10 m.

92-6. *Halichoeres* sp., juvenile (8 cm), Similan Islands, Andaman Sea, 8 m.

92-7. *Halichoeres* sp. (20 cm), Similan Islands, Andaman Sea, 8 m.

92-8. *Halichoeres melanochir*, male (20 cm), Okinawa, 5 m.

## PLATE 93

93-1. *Hemigymnus fasciatus* (6 cm), Vilingilli, Maldive Islands, 6 m.

93-2. *Hemigymnus fasciatus* (30 cm), Mahe, Seychelles, 8 m.

93-3. *Hemigymnus melapterus* (25 cm), Vilingilli, Maldive Islands, 2 m.

93-4. *Hologymnosus annulatus* (22 cm), Mauritius, 12 m.

93-5. *Hologymnosus doliatus*, juvenile (12 cm), Similan Islands, Andaman Sea, 8 m.

93-6. *Hologymnosus doliatus*, female (25 cm), Christmas Island, 12 m.

93-7. *Hologymnosus doliatus*, male (30 cm), Sodwana Bay, South Africa, 16 m.

93-8. *Pterogogus flagelliferus* (10 cm), Mauritius, 20 m.

PLATE 94

94-1. *Labrichthys unilineata*, juvenile (6 cm), Watamu, Kenya, 12 m.
94-2. *Labrichthys unilineata* (20 cm), Vilingilli, Maldive Islands, 12 m.
94-3. *Labropsis xanthonota* (8 cm), Similan Islands, Andaman Sea, 10 m.
94-4. *Larabicus quadrilineatus* (7 cm), Jeddah, Red Sea, 5 m.
94-5. *Macropharyngodon bipartitus* (12 cm), Vilingilli, Maldive Islands, 12 m.
94-6. *Macropharyngodon cyanoguttatus* (14 cm), Mahe, Seychelles, 15 m.
94-7. *Macropharyngodon ornatus* (12 cm), Christmas Island, 15 m.
94-8. *Cheilio inermis* (24 cm), Mahe, Seychelles, 12 m.

PLATE 95

95-1. *Xyrichthys pavo*, juvenile (4 cm), Christmas Island, 4 m.
95-2. *Xyrichthys pavo* (18 cm), Great Barrier Reef, 6 m.
95-3. *Novaculichthys taeniurus* (22 cm), Similan Islands, Andaman Sea, 8 m.
95-4. *Novaculichthys taeniurus*, juvenile (10 cm), Great Barrier Reef, 6 m.
95-5. *Novaculichthys macrolepidotus* (12 cm), Mombasa, Kenya (aquarium photo).
95-6. *Pseudocheilinus evanidus* (8 cm), Vilingilli, Maldive Islands, 10 m.
95-7. *Pseudocheilinus hexataenia* (6 cm), Vilingilli, Maldive Islands, 12 m.
95-8. *Pseudocheilinus octotaenia* (12 cm), Mauritius, 8 m.

PLATE 96

96-1. *Paracheilinus octotaenia* (15 cm), Gulf of Aqaba, Red Sea, 10 m.
96-2. *Pseudocoris* sp. (8 cm), Mauritius, 18 m.
96-3. *Ophthalmolepis lineolatus*, male (20 cm), Recherche Archipelago, Western Australia, 6 m.
96-4. *Ophthalmolepis lineolatus*, female (18 cm), Recherche Archipelago, Western Australia, 8 m.
96-5. *Pseudojuloides erythrops*, female (9 cm), Mauritius (aquarium photo).
96-6. *Pseudojuloides erythrops*, male (13 cm), Mauritius (aquarium photo).
96-7. *Pseudojuloides trifasciatus* (8 cm), Shimoni, Kenya, 2 m.
96-8. *Pseudojuloides cerasinus* (10 cm), Mauritius (aquarium photo).

PLATE 97

97-1. *Pseudolabrus biserialis* (20 cm), Recherche Archipelago, Western Australia, 15 m.
97-2. *Pseudolabrus parilus* (18 cm), Recherche Archipelago, Western Australia, 6 m.
97-3. *Stethojulis albovittatus* (14 cm), Christmas Island, 10 m.
97-4. *Stethojulis strigiventer*, female (10 cm), Rabaul, New Britain, 3 m.
97-5. *Thalassoma amblycephalus*, male (12 cm), Great Barrier Reef, 10 m.
97-6. *Thalassoma amblycephalus*, male (10 cm), Great Barrier Reef, 10 m.
97-7. *Thalassoma commersoni* (20 cm), Mauritius, 12 m.
97-8. *Thalassoma hardwickei* (16 cm), Vilingilli, Maldive Islands, 3 m.

PLATE 98

98-1. *Thalassoma hebraicum* (28 cm), Watamu, Kenya, 12 m.
98-2. *Thalassoma hebraicum* (25 cm), Sodwana Bay, South Africa, 13 m.
98-3. *Thalassoma lunare*, male (20 cm), Watamu, Kenya, 12 m.
98-4. *Thalassoma lutescens* (20 cm), Houtman Abrolhos, Western Australia, 6 m.
98-5. *Thalassoma purpureum* (18 cm), Vilingilli, Maldive Islands, 3 m.
98-6. *Thalassoma ruppelli* (20 cm), Gulf of Aqaba, Red Sea, 6 m.
98-7. *Thalassoma* sp. (16 cm), Mauritius, 10 m.
98-8. *Pseudodax moluccensis* (8 cm), Shimoni, Kenya, 15 m.

PLATE 99

99-1 to 4. *Brachysomophis crocodilinus*, family Ophichthidae (120 cm), Christmas Island, 12 m. This burrowing snake eel waits for passing prey with only its eyes and snout exposed above the sandy surface. When a small fish or crustacean ventures near it quickly emerges from the sand and siezes its victim.
99-5. *Saurida gracilis*, family Synodontidae (18 cm), Mauritius, 4 m.
99-6. *Aulostomus chinensis* (above), family Aulostomidae (50 cm) and *Arothron mappa*, family Tetraodontidae (65 cm), Great Barrier Reef, 8 m. The slender trumpet fish uses the body of this slow-swimming puffer as a shield to sneak up on small fishes.
99-7. Halfbeaks (family Hemiramphidae) feed on clupeids, atherinids, and other small fishes that school near the surface. This photo was taken at Vilingilli, Maldive Islands.
99-8. *Sphyraena flavicauda*, family Sphyraenidae (35 cm), Christmas Island, 12 m.

PLATE 100
100-1. *Gnathanodon speciosus*, family Carangidae (24 cm), Rabaul, New Britain, 12 m.
100-2. *Carangoides fulvoguttatus*, family Carangidae (60 cm), Sodwana Bay, South Africa, 25 m.
100-3. *Caranx melampygus*, family Carangidae (50 cm), Vilingilli, Maldive Islands, 15 m.
100-4. *Plectropomus leopardus*, family Serranidae (80 cm), Vilingilli, Maldive Islands, 15 m.
100-5. *Lutjanus bohar*, family Lutjanidae (50 cm), Great Barrier Reef, 5 m.
100-6. *Gymnosarda unicolor*, family Scombridae (100 cm), Vilingilli, Maldive Islands, 20 m.
100-7. *Carcharhinus amblyrhynchos*, family Carcharhinidae (150 cm), Great Barrier Reef, 10 m.
100-8. *Carcharhinus albomarginata*, family Carcharhinidae (250 cm), Coral Sea, 20 m.

PLATE 101
101-1. *Cetoscarus bicolor*, juvenile (8 cm), Mahe, Seychelles, 8 m.
101-2. *Cetoscarus bicolor*, male (40 cm), Vilingilli, Maldive Islands, 10 m.
101-3. *Hipposcarus harid* (35 cm), Vilingilli, Maldive Islands, 6 m.
101-4. *Scarus gibbus*, male (45 cm), Vilingilli, Maldive Islands, 6 m.
101-5. *Scarus gibbus*, female (40 cm), Vilingilli, Maldive Islands, 5 m.

PLATE 102
102-1. *Scarus prasiognathos*, male (40 cm), Vilingilli, Maldive Islands, 5 m.
102-2. *Scarus niger* (10 cm), Vilingilli, Maldive Islands, 6 m.
102-3. *Scarus niger*, female (30 cm), Similan Islands, Andaman Sea, 8 m.
102-4. *Scarus niger*, male (42 cm), Vilingilli, Maldive Islands, 12 m.
102-5. *Scarus cyanescens* (35 cm), Sodwana Bay, South Africa, 10 m.
102-6. *Scarus psittacus*, male (30 cm), Mombasa, Kenya (aquarium photo).
102-7. *Scarus rubroviolaceus*, male (50 cm), Sodwana Bay, South Africa, 10 m.
102-8. *Scarus rubroviolaceus*, female (40 cm), Sodwana Bay, South Africa, 22 m.

PLATE 103
103-1. *Scarus atrilunula* (32 cm), Sodwana Bay, South Africa, 10 m.
103-2. *Scarus dimidiatus*, female (30 cm), Great Barrier Reef (aquarium photo).
103-3. *Scarus sordidus*, male (35 cm), Vilingilli, Maldive Islands, 3 m.
103-4. *Scarus venosus*, female (30 cm), Houtman Abrolhos, Western Australia, 6 m.
103-5. *Scarus gibbus*, (30 cm), female, Gulf of Aqaba, Red Sea, 10 m.
103-6. *Hipposcarus caudovittatus* (30 cm), Vilingilli, Maldive Islands, 8 m.
103-7. *Scarus ghobban* (32 cm), Mahe, Seychelles, 6 m.
103-8. *Scarus frenatus* (40 cm), Vilingilli, Maldive Islands, 6 m.

PLATE 104
104-1. *Parapercis cephalopunctata*, female (16 cm), Similan Islands, Andaman Sea, 15 m.
104-2. *Parapercis cephalopunctata*, male (20 cm), Similan Islands, Andaman Sea, 10 m.
104-3. *Parapercis bivittata* (13 cm), Vilingilli, Maldive Islands, 35 m.
104-4. *Parapercis haackei* (15 cm), Recherche Archipelago, Western Australia, 10 m.
104-5. *Parapercis polyophthalma* (20 cm), Gulf of Aqaba, Red Sea, 5 m.
104-6. *Parapercis tetracantha* (18 cm), Rabaul, New Britain, 4 m.
104-7. *Parapercis trispilota* (16 cm), Mauritius, 15 m.
104-8. *Parapercis* sp. (possibly the young of *P. cylindrica*) (8 cm), Phuket, Thailand, 8 m.

PLATE 105
105-1. *Aspidontus dussumieri* (8 cm), Mauritius, 25 m.
105-2. *Aspidontus dussumieri* (8 cm), Mauritius, 25 m.
105-3. *Cirripectes variolosus* (8 cm), Similan Islands, Andaman Sea, 6 m.
105-4. *Pereulixia kosiensis* (5 cm), Sodwana Bay, South Africa, 1 m.
105-5. *Plagiotremus tapeinosoma* (10 cm), Coral Sea, 10 m.
105-6. *Meiacanthus mossambicus* (11 cm), Malindi, Kenya, 5 m.
105-7. *Ecsenius* sp. (possibly *oculus*) (5 cm), Christmas Island, 6 m.
105-8. *Ecsenius* sp. (7 cm), Similan Islands, Andaman Sea, 10 m.

## PLATE 106

106-1. *Ecsenius midas*, male (10 cm), Christmas Island, 20 m.
106-2. *Ecsenius midas*, female (8 cm), Christmas Island, 20 m.
106-3. *Ecsenius oculus* (6 cm), Christmas Island, 5 m.
106-4. *Ecsenius oculus* (6 cm), Christmas Island, 5 m.
106-5. *Ecsenius lineatus* (8 cm), Vilingilli, Maldive Islands, 20 m.
106-6. *Ecsenius lineatus* (8 cm), Vilingilli, Maldive Islands, 25 m.
106-7. *Ecsenius nalolo* (5 cm), Vilingilli, Maldive Islands, 4 m.
106-8. *Ecsenius gravieri* (6 cm), Jeddah, Red Sea, 8 m.

## PLATE 107

107-1. *Istiblennius edentulus* (8 cm), Phuket, Thailand, 1 m.
107-2. *Istiblennius periophthalmus* (12 cm), Dampier Archipelago, Western Australia, 4 m.
107-3. *Istiblennius striatomaculatus*, male (10 cm), Kosi Bay, South Africa, 1 m.
107-4. *Istiblennius striatomaculatus*, female (10 cm), Kosi Bay, South Africa, 1 m.
107-5. *Omobranchus elongatus* (7 cm), Shimoni, Kenya, 2 m.
107-6. *Petroscirtes mitratus* (8 cm), Houtman Abrolhos, Western Australia, 6 m.
107-7. *Exallias brevis* (10 cm), Christmas Island, 5 m.
107-8. *Congrogadus subducens* (40 cm), Dampier Archipelago, Western Australia, 5 m.

## PLATE 108

108-1. *Tripterygion* sp. (3 cm), Hikkaduwa, Sri Lanka, 6 m.
108-2. *Tripterygion* sp. (3 cm), Similan Islands, Andaman Sea, 15 m.
108-3. *Enneapterygius* sp. (2.5 cm), Similan Islands, Andaman Sea, 10 m.
108-4. *Enneapterygius* sp. (3 cm), Christmas Island, 12 m.
108-5. *Gunnelichthys curiosus* (8 cm), Vilingilli, Maldive Islands, 40 m.
108-6. *Gunnelichthys monostigma* (10 cm), Great Barrier Reef, 2 m.
108-7. *Malacanthus brevirostris* (18 cm), Shimoni, Kenya, 12 m.
108-8. *Hoplolatilus cuniculus* (12 cm), Mauritius, 20 m.

## PLATE 109

109-1. *Amblyeleotris aurora* (8 cm), Vilingilli, Maldive Islands, 35 m.
109-2. *Amblyeleotris fasciatus* (7 cm), Vilingilli, Maldive Islands, 20 m.
109-3. *Amblyeleotris fontanesii* (9 cm), Rabaul, New Britain, 10 m.
109-4. *Amblyeleotris periophthalmus* (8 cm), Similan Islands, Andaman Sea, 10 m.
109-5. *Amblyeleotris steinitzi* (6 cm), Mahe, Seychelles, 8 m.
109-6. *Amblyeleotris sungami* (7 cm), Mahe, Seychelles, 8 m.
109-7. *Amblyeleotris* sp. (6 cm), Similan Islands, Andaman Sea, 10 m.
109-8. *Amblyeleotris* sp. (10 cm.), Phuket, Thailand, 12 m.

## PLATE 110

110-1. *Amblygobius decussatus* (9 cm), Rabaul, New Britain, 4 m.
110-2. *Amblygobius hectori* (7 cm), Phuket, Thailand, 3 m.
110-3. *Amblygobius nocturnus* (7 cm), Mahe, Seychelles, 10 m.
110-4. *Amblygobius phalaena* (10 cm), Houtman Abrolhos, Western Australia, 6 m.
110-5. *Amblygobius semicinctus* (10 cm), Mauritius, 2 m.
110-6. *Amblygobius sphynx* (12 cm), Rabaul, New Britain, 3 m.
110-7. *Asterropteryx semipunctatus* (6 cm), Great Barrier Reef, 4 m.
110-8. *Bryaninops* sp. (2.5 cm), Similan Islands, Andaman Sea, 6 m.

## PLATE 111

111-1. *Cryptocentrus caeruleomaculatus* (5 cm), Mombasa, Kenya, 10 m.
111-2. *Cryptocentrus cinctus* (7 cm), Phuket, Thailand, 10 m.
111-3. *Cryptocentrus cryptocentrus* (8 cm), Mahe, Seychelles, 10 m.
111-4. *Cryptocentrus fasciatus* (7 cm), Phuket, Thailand, 12 m.
111-5. *Cryptocentrus lutheri* (7 cm), Mombasa, Kenya, 15 m.
111-6. *Cryptocentrus strigilliceps* (5 cm), Great Barrier Reef, 3 m.
111-7. *Ctenogobiops crocineus* (6 cm), Mahe, Seychelles, 6 m.
111-8. *Ctenogobiops feroculus* (8 cm), Rabaul, New Britain, 8 m.

## PLATE 112

112-1. Red coral goby, *Eviota* species, 2 cm TL, Houtman Abrolhos, Western Australia, 15 m.

112-2. Pink spot shrimp goby, *Cryptocentrus obliquus*, 10 cm TL, Rosemary Island, Dampier Archipelago, Western Australia, 3 m.

## PLATE 113

113-1. *Ctenogobiops maculosus* (7 cm), Vilingilli, Maldive Islands, 1 m.

113-2. *Fusigobius neophytus* (6 cm), Mahe, Seychelles, 12 m.

113-3. *Fusigobius* sp. (6 cm), Vilingilli, Maldive Islands, 10 m.

113-4. *Gnatholepis* sp. (5 cm), Phuket, Thailand, 6 m.

113-5. *Gobiodon citrinus* (4 cm), Mahe, Seychelles, 18 m.

113-6. *Nemateleotris magnifica* (6 cm), Christmas Island, 15 m.

113-7. *Nemateleotris decora* (6 cm), Christmas Island, 35 m.

113-8. *Nemateleotris decora* (6 cm), Great Barrier Reef, 30 m.

## PLATE 114

114-1. *Periophthalmus koelruteri* (4-10 cm), Mombasa, Kenya (aquarium photo).

114-2. *Pleurosicya* sp. (2.5 cm), Similan Islands, Andaman Sea, 5 m.

114-3. *Ptereleotris evides* (3 cm), Vilingilli, Maldive Islands, 3 m.

114-4. *Ptereleotris evides* (12 cm), Vilingilli, Maldive Islands, 10 m.

114-5. *Ptereleotris heteropterus* (9 cm), Vilingilli, Maldive Islands, 35 m.

114-6. *Ptereleotris microlepis* (10 cm), Rabaul, New Britain, 2 m.

114-7. *Vanderhorstia ambonoro* (8 cm), Rabaul, New Britain, 3 m.

114-8. *Vanderhorstia ornatissima* (7 cm), Vilingilli, Maldive Islands, 2 m.

## PLATE 115

115-1. *Valenciennea longipinnis* (13 cm), Great Barrier Reef, 6 m.

115-2. *Valenciennea helsdingeni* (15 cm), Christmas Island, 16 m.

115-3. *Valenciennea puellaris* (12 cm), North West Cape, Western Australia, 8 m.

115-4. *Valenciennea puellaris* (12 cm), Phuket, Thailand, 15 m.

115-5. *Valenciennea sexguttatus* (12 cm), Phuket, Thailand, 4 m.

115-6. *Valenciennea strigatus* (12 cm), Shimoni, Kenya, 8 m.

115-7. *Valenciennea muralis* (8 cm), Phuket, Thailand, 10 m.

115-8. *Priolepis cinctus* (4 cm), Mauritius (aquarium photo).

## PLATE 116

116-1. *Auxis thazard*, frigate tuna.

116-2. *Euthynnus affinis*, kawakawa.

116-3. *Katsuwonus pelamis*, skipjack tuna.

116-4. *Cybiosarda elegans*, leaping bonito.

116-5. *Thunnus alalunga*, albacore.

116-6. *Thunnus albacares*, yellowfin tuna.

116-7. *Thunnus maccoyii*, southern bluefin tuna.

116-8. *Thunnus obesus*, bigeye tuna.

116-9. *Thunnus tonggol*, longtail tuna.

116-10. *Acanthocybium solandri*, wahoo.

## PLATE 117

117-1. *Gymnosarda unicolor*, dogtooth tuna.

117-2. *Grammatorcynus bicarinatus*.

117-3. *Rastrelliger kanagurta*.

117-4. *Sarda orientalis*, striped bonito.

117-5. *Scomber japonicus*, chub mackerel.

117-6. *Scomberomorus commerson*, narrow-barred Spanish mackerel.

117-7. *Scomberomorus lineolatus*, streaked Spanish mackerel.

117-8. *Scomberomorus guttatus*, king Spanish mackerel.

117-9. *Scomberomorus queenslandicus*, Queensland Spanish mackerel.

117-10. *Scomberomorus semifasciatus*, broad barred Spanish mackerel.

117-11. *Scomberomorus niphonius*, Japanese Spanish mackerel.

## PLATE 118
118-1. *Xiphias gladius*, swordfish.
118-2. *Istiophorus platypterus*, sailfish.
118-3. *Tetrapturus audax*, striped marlin.
118-4. *Makaira mazara*, blue marlin.
118-5. *Makaira indica*, black marlin.
118-6. *Coryphaena hippurus*, dolphinfish.
118-7. *Tetrapturus angustirostris*, shortbill spearfish.

## PLATE 119
119-1. *Trichonotus filamentosus*, family Trichonotidae (15 cm), Rabaul, New Britain, 15 m. The male sand-lance presents a peacock-like display to another male encroaching on its territory.
119-2. *Cheilinus bimaculatus*, family Labridae (9 cm), Watamu, Kenya, 15 m. Ritual behavioral patterns such as jaw-locking is occasionally seen in wrasses and damselfishes.
119-3. *Meiacanthus grammistes*, family Blenniidae (10 cm), Great Barrier Reef, 10 m. Sabertooth blennies occupy rocky burrows and defend well-defined territories in the vicinity of their lair. The male individual with erected fins is responding to the intrusion of a conspecific fish of the same sex.
119-4. *Gymnothorax breedeni*, family Muraenidae (90 cm), Christmas Island, 15 m. Most moray eels will not attack humans unless provoked. However, this recently discovered species is extremely aggressive toward intruders. Both authors received bites while photographing at Christmas Island and the Maldives.
119-5. *Canthigaster epilamprus*, family Tetraodontidae (8 cm), Christmas Island, 20 m. Male sharpnose puffers frequently engage in brief skirmishes, particularly in the presence of females. The erect flap of skin on the belly is only apparent during fighting and courtship.

## PLATE 120
120-1. *Acanthurus bleekeri* (40 cm), Sodwana Bay, South Africa, 10 m.
120-2. *Acanthurus glaucopareius* (20 cm), Christmas Island, 10 m.
120-3. *Acanthurus leucosternon* (20 cm), Similan Islands, Andaman Sea, 10 m.
120-4. *Acanthurus guttatus* (20 cm), Christmas Island, 5 m.
120-5. *Acanthurus leucosternon* (24 cm), Vilingilli, Maldive Islands, 3 m.

## PLATE 121
121-1. *Acanthurus nigrofuscus* (15 cm), Christmas Island, 2 m.
121-2. *Acanthurus olivaceus* (25 cm), Great Barrier Reef (aquarium photo).
121-3. *Acanthurus pyroferus*, yellow juvenile phase (10 cm), Great Barrier Reef, 6 m.
121-4. *Acanthurus pyroferus* (22 cm), Rabaul, New Britain, 10 m. The juvenile stage of this surgeonfish often mimics various species of *Centropyge* angelfishes.
121-5. *Acanthurus sohal* (30 cm), Muscat, Oman, 2 m.
121-6. *Acanthurus tennenti* (20 cm), Watamu, Kenya, 12 m.
121-7. *Acanthurus thompsoni* (22 cm), Similan Islands, Andaman Sea, 15 m.
121-8. *Acanthurus xanthopterus* (25 cm), Mahe, Seychelles, 10 m.

## PLATE 122
122-1. *Acanthurus nigricaudus* (24 cm), Christmas Island, 8 m.
122-2. *Acanthurus lineatus* (8 cm), Christmas Island, 10 m.
122-3. *Acanthurus maculiceps* (30 cm), Christmas Island, 8 m.
122-4. *Acanthurus* sp. (possibly juvenile of *A. mata*) (9 cm), Mauritius, 2 m.
122-5. *Ctenochaetus strigosus* (3 cm), Christmas Island, 5 m.

## PLATE 123

123-1. *Ctenochaetus strigosus* (20 cm), Shimoni, Kenya, 6 m.
123-2. *Ctenochaetus strigosus* (3 cm), Christmas Island, 8 m.
123-3. *Paracanthurus hepatus* (18 cm), Sodwana Bay, South Africa, 22 m.
123-4. *Naso tuberosus* (65 cm), Great Barrier Reef, 10 m.
123-5. *Naso brevirostris* (35 cm), Vilingilli, Maldive Islands, 6 m.
123-6. *Naso lituratus* (29 cm), Vilingilli, Maldive Islands, 3 m.
123-7. *Naso vlamingi* (55 cm), Vilingilli, Maldive Islands, 5 m.
123-8. *Naso vlamingi* (55 cm), Vilingilli, Maldive Islands, 6 m.

## PLATE 124

124-1. *Zebrasoma scopas* (13 cm), Vilingilli, Maldive Islands, 8 m.
124-2. *Zebrasoma gemmatum* (8 cm), Mauritius, 25 m.
124-3. *Zebrasoma scopas* (6 cm), Mauritius, 2 m.
124-4. *Zebrasoma desjardini* (16 cm), Mahe, Seychelles, 7 m.
124-5. *Zebrasoma desjardini* (4 cm), Mauritius, 2 m.
124-6. *Zanclus cornutus* (23 cm), Vilingilli, Maldive Islands, 20 m.
124-7. *Zebrasoma xanthurus* (12 cm), Muscat, Oman, 6 m.

## PLATE 125

125-1. Two–barred rabbitfish, *Siganus doliatus* about 25 cm TL, in 12 meters depth, North West Cape.
125-2. Three-spot rabbitfish, *Siganus trispilos* 22 cm TL, from 4 meters depth, North West Cape.

## PLATE 126

126-1. *Lo magnifica* (25 cm), Similan Islands, Andaman Sea, 12 m.
126-2. *Siganus canaliculatus* (12 cm), Mauritius, 2 m.
126-3. *Siganus guttatus* (30 cm), Phuket, Thailand, 8 m.
126-4. *Siganus guttatus?* (35 cm), Hikkaduwa, Sri Lanka, 12 m.
126-5. *Siganus corallinus* (30 cm), Great Barrier Reef, 10 m.
126-6. *Siganus javus?* (30 cm), Great Barrier Reef, 8 m.
126-7. *Siganus puelloides* (20 cm), Vilingilli, Maldive Islands, 10 m.
126-8. *Siganus stellatus* (25 cm), Vilingilli, Maldive Islands, 5 m.

## PLATE 127

127-1. *Abalistes stellaris* (8 cm), Ambon, Indonesia, 10 m.
127-2. *Balistapus undulatus* (25 cm), Vilingilli, Maldive Islands, 5 m.
127-3. *Balistoides conspicillum* (28 cm), Vilingilli, Maldive Islands, 5 m.
127-4. *Melichthys vidua* (22 cm), Great Barrier Reef, 10 m.
127-5. *Melichthys indicus* (30 cm), Vilingilli, Maldive Islands, 4 m.
127-6. *Melichthys indicus* (14 cm), Christmas Island, 5 m.
127-7. *Xanthichthys auromarginatus*, female (20 cm), Christmas Island, 20 m.
127-8. *Xanthichthys auromarginatus*, male (22 cm), Christmas Island, 20 m.

## PLATE 128

128-1. *Pseudobalistes fuscus* (18 cm), Vilingilli, Maldive Islands, 30 m.
128-2. *Pseudobalistes flavimarginatus* (6 cm), Great Barrier Reef, 3 m.
128-3. *Pseudobalistes fuscus* (35 cm), Vilingilli, Maldive Islands, 20 m.
128-4. *Pseudobalistes viridescens* (50 cm), Vilingilli, Maldive Islands, 10 m.
128-5. *Rhinecanthus aculeatus* (20 cm), Vilingilli, Maldive Islands, 2 m.
128-6. *Rhinecanthus assasi* (20 cm), Gulf of Aqaba, Red Sea, 3 m.
128-7. *Rhinecanthus rectangulus* (10 cm), Christmas Island, 5 m.

## PLATE 129
129-1. *Sufflamen bursa* (18 cm), Christmas Island, 10 m.
129-2. *Sufflamen chrysoptera* (20 cm), Vilingilli, Maldive Islands, 8 m.
129-3. *Sufflamen frenatus* (6 cm), Rabaul, New Britain, 15 m.
129-4. *Odonus niger* (21 cm), Vilingilli, Maldive Islands, 15 m.
129-5. *Amanses scopas* (25 cm), Vilingilli, Maldive Islands, 6 m.
129-6. *Cantherhines paradalis* (15 cm), Vilingilli, Maldive Islands, 5 m.
129-7. *Cantherhines dumerili* (25 cm), Christmas Island, 8 m.
129-8. *Cantherhines dumerili* (10 cm), Mombasa, Kenya (aquarium photo).

## PLATE 130
130-1. *Meuchenia flavolineata* (25 cm), Recherche Archipelago, Western Australia, 6 m.
130-2. *Meuchenia galeii* (35 cm), Recherche Archipelago, Western Australia, 10 m.
130-3. *Meuchenia hippocrepis* (25 cm), Recherche Archipelago, Western Australia, 5 m.
130-4. *Oxymonacanthus longirostris* (6 cm), Mahe, Seychelles, 5 m.
130-5. *Pervagor melanocephalus* (8 cm), Christmas Island, 10 m.
130-6. *Scobinichthys granulatus* (13 cm), Geographe Bay, Western Australia, 10 m.
130-7. *Chaetoderma penicilligera* (7 cm), Cebu, Philippines, 5 m.
130-8. *Alutera scripta* (60 cm), Rabaul, New Britain, 10 m.

## PLATE 131
131-1. *Anaplocapros lenticularis* (8 cm), Houtman Abrolhos, Western Australia, 10 m.
131-2. *Aracana aurita* (22 cm), Geographe Bay, Western Australia, 10 m.
131-3. *Lactoria cornutus* (15 cm), Mombasa, Kenya (aquarium photo).
131-4. *Anaplocapros lenticularis* (14 cm), Cockburn Sound, Western Australia, 10 m.

## PLATE 132
132-1. *Ostracion cubicus* (15 cm), Vilingilli, Maldive Islands, 10 m.
132-2. *Ostracion cubicus* (12 cm), Aliwal Shoal, South Africa, 20 m.
132-3. *Ostracion meleagris*, male (12 cm), Christmas Island, 12 m.
132-4. *Ostracion meleagris*, female (12 cm), Mauritius, 10 m.
132-5. *Ostracion trachys* (15 cm), Mauritius, 15 m.
132-6. *Tetrasomus gibbosus* (8 cm), Gulf of Aqaba, Red Sea, 4 m.
132-7. *Lactoria fornasini* (8 cm), Miyake Jima, 10 m.
132-8. *Lactoria diaphanus* (10 cm), Miyake Jima, Japan, 10 m.

## PLATE 133
133-1. *Arothron hispidus* (25 cm), Houtman Abrolhos, Western Australia, 5 m.
133-2. *Arothron meleagris* (30 cm), Mauritius, 12 m.
133-3. *Arothron nigropunctatus* (30 cm), Christmas Island, 12 m.
133-4. *Arothron nigropunctatus* (30 cm), Christmas Island, 20 m.
133-5. *Arothron stellatus* (30 cm), Mauritius, 15 m.
133-6. *Arothron* sp. (30 cm), Aliwal Shoal, South Africa, 20 m.
133-7. *Omegophora cyanopunctata* (12 cm), Recherche Archipelago, Western Australia, 15 m.
133-8. *Torquigener* sp. (15 cm), Gulf of Aqaba, Red Sea, 5 m.

## PLATE 134

134-1. *Canthigaster amboinensis* (3 cm), Mauritius, 3 m.

134-2. *Canthigaster amboinensis* (11 cm), Christmas Island, 4 m.

134-3. *Canthigaster bennetti* (6 cm), Shimoni, Kenya, 2 m.

134-4. *Canthigaster coronatus* (6 cm), Mauritius, 12 m.

134-5. *Canthigaster epilamprus* (7 cm), Christmas Island, 20 m.

134-6. *Canthigaster janthinoptera* (8 cm), Christmas Island, 10 m.

134-7. *Canthigaster leopardus* (6 cm), Christmas Island, 35 m.

134-8. *Canthigaster smithae* (8 cm), Mauritius, 30 m.


## PLATE 135

135-1. *Canthigaster natalensis* (10 cm), Sodwana Bay, South Africa, 10 m.

135-2. *Canthigaster natalensis*, male (10 cm), Sodwana Bay, South Africa, 15 m.

135-3. *Canthigaster solandri* (10 cm), Malindi, Kenya, 15 m.

135-4. *Canthigaster tyleri* (7 cm), Christmas Island (aquarium photo).

135-5. *Chilomycterus affinis* (30 cm), Miyake Jima, Japan, 5 m.

135-6. *Chilomycterus orbicularis* (14 cm), Batangas, Philippines, 10 m.

135-7. *Diodon hystrix* (50 cm), Christmas Island, 12 m.

135-8. *Diodon nicthemerus* (40 cm), Houtman Abrolhos, Western Australia, 6 m.


## PLATE 136

136-1. *Amphiprion nigripes*, family Pomacentridae (9 cm), Vilingilli, Maldive Islands, 5 m. The parent anemonefish tend their nest of eggs. The eggs are periodically fanned with the pectoral fins and dead or diseased eggs removed by mouth.

136-2. *Nemanthias carburyi*, family Serranidae (13 cm), Aliwal Shoal, South Africa, 10 m. Male fairy basslets are brighter colored than females (background), particularly during courtship activities.

136-3. *Valenciennea helsdingeni* (15 cm), Rabaul, New Britain, 15 m.

136-4. *Valenciennea helsdingeni*, family Gobiidae (15 cm), Rabaul, New Britain, 15 m. This goby lays eggs in a sandy burrow. The parent fish continually remove debris and reinforce the nest site during incubation.

136-5. *Nemateleotris magnifica*, family Gobiidae (8 cm), Vilingilli, Maldive Islands, 20 m. Gobies often form permanent reproductive pairs that share a common burrow.

136-6. *Bryaninops* sp., family Gobiidae (2 cm), Great Barrier Reef, 10 m. This small goby lives on the surface of sea whips and other gorgonians. It deposits eggs on the cylindrical stalks of its invertebrate host. The parents guard the nest (visible to the right of the fish) until hatching.

136-7. *Stegastes nigricans*, family Pomacentridae (12 cm), Mauritius, 2 m. Normally the male of this damselfish is uniformly brown but during courtship and nest guarding it assumes the pattern seen here. These colors can be switched on or off in an instant.

136-8. *Dascyllus trimaculatus*, family Pomacentridae (10 cm), Christmas Island, 5 m. This damselfish pair is spawning a nest of eggs on a rocky surface. The white ovipositor or egg tube of the darker female is clearly visible. Males are generally similar in color to females except during courtship and spawning.

## PLATE 137

137-1. *Apogon cyanosoma*, family Apogonidae (8 cm), Great Barrier Reef, 6 m. The egg mass is clearly evident in the mouth of this male cardinalfish.

137-2. *Cheilodipterus lineatus*, family Apogonidae (16 cm), Mahe, Seychelles, 8 m. Cardinalfishes are one of few marine fishes that exhibit the unusual habit of mouth-brooding. The gular region of this male is greatly swollen with eggs.

137-3. *Dunckerocampus multiannulatus*, family Syngnathidae (15 cm), Mauritius, 8 m. The male pipefish broods its eggs either in a pouch or in an exposed position on the belly or under the tail. A row of tiny spherical eggs is evident in the photo.

137-4. *Lutjanus gibbus*, family Lutjanidae (35 cm), Vilingilli, Maldive Islands, 12 m. The trailing filament on the individual at the lower right is a meter-long piece of fishing line. Snappers are a favorite food fish throughout the Indian Ocean.

137-5. *Heniochus acuminatus*, family Chaetodontidae (20 cm), Sodwana Bay, South Africa, 10 m. This butterflyfish normally has a single dorsal fin filament, but extremely rare individuals have two or even three.

137-6. *Heniochus diphreutes*, family Chaetodontidae (16 cm), Vilingilli, Maldive Islands, 5 m.

137-7. A rare angelfish (family Pomacanthidae) hybrid of *Centropyge eibli* and *C. flavissimus* (7 cm), Christmas Island, 19 m. A small number of marine fish hybrids have been reported, most of them involving butterflyfishes and angelfishes.

137-8. Hybrid butterflyfish (family Chaetodontidae), a cross of *Chaetodon guttatissimus* and *C. punctatofasciatus* (15 cm), Christmas Island, 12 m.

## PLATE 138

138-1 to 5. *Lactoria fornasini*, family Ostraciontidae (10 cm), Miyake Jima, Japan, 8 m. The spawning sequence shown here is that of a typical open-water spawner.

138-6 to 8. *Gymnothorax boschi*, family Muraenidae (40 cm), Batangas, Philippines. Rare photos that show a number of males spawning with a swollen, egg-filled female (center).

## PLATE 139

139-1. *Platycephalus crocodilus* (50 cm), Watamu, Kenya, 20 m.

139-2. *Platycephalus haackei* (40 cm), Recherche Archipelago, Western Australia, 5 m.

139-3. *Aulopus purpurissatus* (16 cm), Recherche Archipelago, Western Australia, 15 m.

139-4. *Aulopus purpurissatus* (30 cm), Recherche Archipelago, Western Australia, 10 m.

139-5. *Saurida gracila* (14 cm), Mauritius, 2 m.

139-6. *Synodus jaculum* (12 cm), Mauritius, 25 m.

139-7. *Synodus variegatus* (6 cm), Christmas Island, 10 m.

139-8. *Synodus variegatus* (12 cm), Vilingilli, Maldive Islands, 8 m.

## PLATE 140

140-1. *Trichonotus setiger* (18 cm), Batangas, Philippines, 3 m.

140-2. Close up of head of *Trichonotus setiger*.

140-3. *Dactyloptena orientalis*, family Dactylopteridae (20 cm), Batangas, Philippines, 3 m. When viewed from above the awesome outstretched "wings" (pectoral fins) of the sea robin serves to discourage potential predators.

140-4. *Synchiropis splendidus* (5 cm), Great Barrier Reef, 4 m.

140-5. *Synchiropis marmoratus* (8 cm), Mauritius, 25 m.

140-6. *Synchiropis picturatus* (7 cm), Dampier Archipelago, Western Australia (aquarium photo).

140-7. *Synchiropis stellatus* (4 cm), Vilingilli, Maldive Islands, 25 m.

140-8. *Synchiropis* sp. (4 cm), Shimoni, Kenya, 15 m.

## PLATE 141

141-1. *Centroberyx lineatus* (20 cm), Recherche Archipelago, Western Australia, 16 m.

141-2. *Gerres oyena* (20 cm), Kosi Bay, South Africa, 3 m.

141-3. An undescribed species of clingfish (Gobiesocidae) (3 cm), Recherche Archipelago, Western Australia, 25 m.

141-4. *Diademichthys lineatus* (7 cm), Rabaul, New Britain, 6 m.

141-5. *Lepadichthys caritus* (4 cm), Christmas Island, 15 m.

141-6. *Plotosus lineatus* (8 cm), Mauritius, 6 m.

141-7. *Priacanthus cruentatus* (18 cm), Sodwana Bay, South Africa, 15 m.

141-8. *Priacanthus hamrur* (25 cm), Mauritius, 12 m.

## PLATE 142

142-1. *Antennarius analis* (2 cm), Christmas Island (aquarium photo).

142-2. *Antennarius moluccensis* (22 cm), Mauritius, 2 m.

142-3. *Antennarius oligospilos* (10 cm), Mombasa, Kenya (aquarium photo).

142-4. *Monocentrus japonicus*, family Monocentridae (8 cm), Mauritius, 10 m. The strange pineconefish is a nocturnal predator that shelters in caves during the day.

142-5. *Pegasus draconis*, family Pegasidae (5 cm), Okinawa (aquarium photo). The sea moth is a bottom dweller with bony armor similar to that found on pipefishes.

## PLATE 143

143-1. Bridled weed whiting, *Siphonognathus radiatus*, 12 cm TL, Cockburn Sound, Western Australia, 4 m.

143-2. Rainbowfish, *Odax acroptilus*, male, 16 cm TL, Houtman Abrolhos, Western Australia, 10 m.

## PLATE 144

144-1. *Rhinobatos blochii* (100 cm), Durban Aquarium, South Africa.

144-2. *Centriscus strigatus*, family Centriscidae (16 cm), Great Barrier Reef, 5 m. The razorfish always swims in this vertical position. It shelters among branching coral or between the spines of sea urchins.

144-3. *Rhiniodon typus*, family Rhiniodontidae (400 cm), Great Barrier Reef. The whale shark is the largest fish inhabiting the world's seas. Although it is reported to reach a length of 20 m, most reliable records indicate a maximum size of 10-12 m. This species feeds on plankton and is not considered dangerous.

144-4. *Echeneis naucrates* (45 cm), Great Barrier Reef, 10 m.

144-5. *Siphonognathus caninis* (10 cm), Recherche Archipelago, Western Australia, 12 m.

144-6. *Aulostomus chinensis* (50 cm), Christmas Island, 12 m.

# Chapter Twenty-six

# *Gobies*

If one were to select the single most successful coral reef family from an evolutionary standpoint, the Gobiidae would certainly deserve the number one rating. Gobies are literally everywhere on tropical or subtropical reefs and usually in large numbers. They have successfully penetrated a wide range of habitats, from rich living coral reefs to vast barren stretches of silty or sandy bottom. A number of species have also invaded estuarine and freshwater habitats, often being found hundreds of kilometers inland. Conservative estimates on the total number of gobies exceed 1600 species. In the Indian Ocean region alone there are perhaps as many as 400 species belonging to at least 90 genera, and new species are still being discovered at an astonishing rate. The large number of genera and species makes this family one of the most difficult ones for taxonomists. Relatively few of the genera have been adequately worked on by specialists, and most of the larger goby groups are in desperate need of study.

Why are there so many gobies? This question is not easily answered, but one factor may be that the probable center for evolution of the family is the species-rich Indo-Malayan Archipelago. Because of relatively stable temperature regimes over long periods of geologic time coupled with a wide diversity of habitat conditions in this region, gobiid evolution has had an opportunity to proceed at an accelerated rate.

Although gobies exhibit a great deal of diversity with regard to their overall body size and shape, most species are somewhat elongate and are characterized by the possession of a peculiar disc-like structure composed of the fused pelvic fins. This apparatus is useful for perching on soft, muddy bottoms and possibly is indicative that ancestral gobies were adapted to this type of habitat. A number of species, however, lack the pelvic disc and have more or less "normal" pelvic fins that are separate. Most of these species have forsaken the typical bottom-dwelling mode and frequently swim for long periods above the bottom. Common examples of gobies with split pelvic fins are the members of the genera *Nemateleotris* and *Ptereleotris*. The majority of gobies are very small in size, usually under 10 cm, with many species under 5 or 6 cm. In fact, the world's smallest fish is a species of goby belonging to the genus *Pandaka*. It attains sexual maturity at a length of under 1 cm!

The richest habitats for gobies are characterized by soft silty or sandy bottoms. Rubble areas and dead coral reefs also harbor large numbers of these fishes. The dependence on sand or silt substrata is at least partly dictated by their requirements for shelter and reproduction. The majority of gobies construct their own burrows or use abandoned burrows in the soft bottom. Typically the bottom-dwelling species occur either solitarily or in pairs, seldom straying far from the entrance of the burrow during foraging activities. If danger threatens they hastily retreat to their lair. The food of gobies is extremely variable. Virtually all small, edible items of plant and animal matter are consumed. A large number of species feed on various crustaceans including crabs, shrimps, ostracods, amphipods, isopods, and copepods. The last item is particularly favored by the midwater feeders such as *Nemateleotris* and *Ptereleotris*. Other common food items include algae, polychaetes, foraminifera, gastropods, pelecypods, echinoderms, small fishes, and insects.

Perhaps the most interesting of all reef gobies are the species of *Cryptocentrus, Ctenogobiops, Vanderhorstia,* and various related genera that live in association with alpheid shrimps. The shrimp excavates and continuously maintains the burrow and appears to gain at least some measure of protection from predation by the presence of its fish neighbor. The goby stands on the alert at the entrance to the burrow and warns the shrimp of approaching danger. Experiments indicate that the shrimps have extremely poor vision.

The large majority of gobies are not brightly colored but exhibit a wide range of browns and tans often overlaid with darker markings. Because of the lack of color they are not regarded highly by most aquarists in spite of their small size, interesting behavior, and ability to acclimate easily to captivity. However, there are bound to be colorful exceptions in a family as large as this one. For example, the three members of the genus *Nemateleotris,* sometimes called firefishes, are among the most beautiful members of the reef community. Their brilliant colors, graceful swimming behavior, and pennant-like dorsal fin make them a favorite with aquarists and underwater photographers.

Typically gobies lay their eggs in clusters on the bottom and the nests are usually tended by the parents until hatching, which requires several days. Gobies are one of the few groups that have been successfully bred in captivity.

Gobies of the genus *Periophthalmus* are known as mudskippers and are found in large numbers in estuaries and mangrove creeks. They are most often seen lying completely out of water on mud banks. Mudskippers are capable of spending long periods out of water and appear to respire at least partially via their moist skin. They move quickly in the direction of the nearest water with a unique hopping or skipping motion when disturbed.

# Chapter Twenty-seven

# *Territoriality*

A number of fishes found on coral reefs and their immediate vicinity roam over relatively large areas in search of food and mates. Many of these travel the same approximate route day after day on a particular reef or over a limited secton of a larger reef. Such fishes are commonly referred to as home-ranging species; in other words, they roam more or less freely over a circumscribed home area. Another major category of bottom-dwelling fishes consists of species that usually are restricted to relatively small areas (several square meters or less) and actively defend the boundaries of their territory, particularly against encroaching members of the same species. Perhaps the best examples of territoriality in reef fishes are the benthic species of damselfishes belonging to the family Pomacentridae. Many of these feed largely on algal matter within the boundaries of their territory, which is usually centered on a coral head, rocky outcrop, or some other form of shelter. The territory is defended not only against other damselfishes but against other algal-feeding species such as surgeonfishes and parrotfishes. The damselfish will confront an intruder several times its own size and drive it away with a series of vigorous bites and charges. Even a gigantic human intruder is not immune to these attacks, which in most damsels are accompanied by clearly audible clicking-type noises.

Certain damselfishes, such as members of the genus *Chromis*, and other reef fishes may be basically home-ranging over most of their life cycle but become strongly territorial during courtship and spawning activities. This is particularly true of species that prepare nests and attach their eggs to the substrate, for example the gobies, blennies, and damselfishes. The reproductive habits of the latter group have been particularly well studied and are discussed later.

Courtship activity and territorial boundary confrontations are often accompanied by dramatic threat displays and outright aggressive behavior. The males of various damselfishes and wrasses sometimes engage in prolonged bouts of jaw-locking in an effort to win the favors of a nearby female. Territorial fishes often exhibit ritual courtship and aggressive displays characterized by the erection of the dorsal fin. In some species this structure is developed into prolonged filaments that greatly enhance the display. For example, the males of some basslets (Anthiinae), sandlances (Trichonotidae), and wrasses (Labridae) exhibit this feature.

# Chapter Twenty-eight

# Surgeonfishes and Rabbitfishes

The surgeonfishes (family Acanthuridae) are extremely common reef-dwellers occurring worldwide in tropical seas. Five genera reside in the Indo-Pacific region. These include *Acanthurus*, *Naso*, *Ctenochaetus*, *Zebrasoma*, and *Paracanthurus*. They are laterally compressed fishes, usually ovate in shape, with a small mouth and single dorsal fin. Acanthurids derive their common name from the bony, knife-like structure at the middle of the tail base that is reminiscent of a surgeon's scalpel. This weapon, apparently a defensive one, is razor-sharp and thus capable of inflicting deep lacerations if the fish are carelessly handled. At least one species, *Acanthurus lineatus*, is reported to have a painful venom associated with the spine. In the genus *Naso* there are one or two spines on each side of the tail base that are immobile, but in the other tropical genera the spines fold into a narrow groove and are erected only when the fish becomes agitated.

The genus *Acanthurus* is by far the largest of the family and contains 33 species. All but the four Atlantic Ocean species are found in the Indo-Pacific. About 20 are present in the Indian Ocean. They are medium-sized fishes, and some of the members of the genus, such as *A. leucosternon* and *A. lineatus*, are among the most colorful fishes to be found on coral reefs. Although they are eaten in many localities, the flesh of surgeonfishes is not particularly tasty. It has a strong flavor typical of many plant-feeding fishes.

The members of this genus sometimes form huge shoals composed of several hundred individuals that graze on filamentous algae. This type of mass feeding appears to be an effective strategy for entering the territories of bottom-dwelling fishes such as pomacentrids, which are able to drive away only one or two intruders at a time but are simply overwhelmed when these mass invasions take place. At least two members of the genus exhibit behavior that is atypical. Thompson's Surgeon (*A. thompsoni*) has forsaken the normal algal diet and forms schools that feed on plankton high above the bottom in outer reef areas. Similar behavior is exhibited by some of the *Naso* surgeons. Another species, *A. lineatus*, has the unusual habit of establishing a territory that it guards mainly from intruding conspecifics. It is primarily a solitary fish, unlike most of the other species, which are often seen in aggregations.

The species of *Naso* are sometimes referred to as unicornfishes because of the bony extension that protrudes from the snout and forehead of some species. This structure is extremely well developed in the adults of *N. brachycentron*, *N. brevirostris*, and *N. unicornis*, where it may be up to several inches in length. This group contains some of the largest members of the family, with a maximum size of about 60 cm being attained by *N. unicornis* and *N. tuberosus*. The males of *N. vlamingi* are more colorful than the females and are capable of bright displays during courtship activities.

The remaining genera contain relatively few Indian Ocean representatives but are nevertheless common on coral reefs. *Ctenochaetus* surgeons are similar in general appearance to *Acanthurus* but differ by having numerous movable teeth with expanded tips that are curved inward. The genus contains seven species, two of which are commonly found in the Indian Ocean (*C. striatus* and *C. strigosus*). Species of the genus *Zebrasoma* are sometimes called sailfin tangs because of their well developed, sail-like dorsal fin. This structure is especially prominent in *Z. desjardini* (and *Z. veliferum* of the Pacific). The genus contains seven species, four of which reside on Indian Ocean—Red Sea reefs. One of these, *Z. gemmatum*, is considered to be extremely rare, with a distribution limited to Mauritius, Reunion, and Madagascar. *Paracanthurus hepatus* is the sole member of its genus. It is one of the most vividly marked members of the family, and juveniles are highly prized as aquarium fishes. The species usually is encountered in small aggregations in rich coral reef areas. They apparently feed on plankton in midwater and if disturbed quickly seek shelter on the bottom among dense growths of branching coral. Juveniles are sometimes collected by bringing the smaller coral heads to the surface and shaking the concealed fish out into a bucket.

The Moorish Idol (*Zanclus cornutus*) is closely related to the surgeonfishes and, in fact, some authors have included it in that family although it is often considered as the sole representative of the family Zanclidae. It's highly contrasted color pattern and graceful shape are responsible for its universal praise among aquarists and coral reef enthusiasts. It is common on most coral reefs and is widely distributed in the Indo-Pacific from the coast of Central America westward to East Africa and the Red Sea.

The rabbitfishes of the family Siganidae are also closely allied to the surgeonfishes. The group is restricted to the tropical Indo-West Pacific and contains approximately 25 species, of which about half are common on Indian Ocean reefs. All belong to the genus *Siganus*, except a single species of *Lo* (*L. magnifica*) found in the eastern Indian Ocean. They are generally similar to surgeons in overall body shape, but are easily differentiated by the presence of two pelvic and seven anal fin spines (compared with one pelvic and two or three anal spines in Acanthuridae). The fin spines of rabbitfishes have poison glands associated with them, and therefore these animals should be handled with great caution, preferably with thick gloves. They are capable of inflicting painful wounds that may require special medical treatment. Most of the species appear to be algal feeders. Several species exhibit bright color patterns that usually include yellow. The colorful siganids tend to be solitary or pair- forming in habit in contrast to the drably colored species that are often encountered in large grazing aggregations. The latter sometimes form mixed schools with surgeonfishes.

# Chapter Twenty-nine

# *Triggerfishes and Filefishes*

Triggerfishes (family Balistidae) and filefishes (family Monacanthidae) are close relatives, so close that some taxonomic specialists lump them together in a single family. The two groups are readily separated, however, on the basis of overall shape and the structure of the spinous dorsal fin. Triggerfishes tend to be stouter (i.e., more robust) and have the first dorsal fin composed of three spines, the first of which is smooth to the touch and only moderately elongate. Typically they are oval shaped, somewhat reminiscent of a football. Filefishes, on the other hand, tend to be more laterally compressed (i.e., thinner) and vary tremendously in shape from nearly circular to extremely elongate, almost pencil-like (as in *Anacanthus*). Moreover, the first dorsal fin is composed of a single elongate spine often bearing horny barbs and there is a rudimentary second spine at its base. There is also a difference in the outer body surface; triggerfishes are covered with large, hard, scute-like scales, whereas filefishes have very small scales armed with one or more tiny spines that give the skin a velvety or sandpaper-like texture. Both groups have a relatively small mouth with relatively few teeth. The jaws are incredibly strong and capable of inflicting painful bites.

Triggerfishes are predominantly tropical reef-dwellers occurring worldwide. Most of the species are confined to the Indo-Pacific region. The Indian Ocean is the home of approximately 20 species. Perhaps the best known of these are the Clown Trigger (*Balistoides conspicillum*) and the Rectangular Trigger (*Rhinecanthus rectangulus*). The exquisite markings of the former species are responsible for its great popularity with aquarists. In the past prices of over $200 have been paid

for a single specimen! The Rectangular Trigger owes much of its popularity to the Hawaiian name of — Humuhumunukunukuapuaa. Juveniles of this species and several other triggers exhibit ornate patterns and are good aquarium pets although they may prove quarrelsome if kept with other species.

Triggerfishes are generally solitary in habit, but members of the genera *Melichthys* and *Odonus*, commonly known as the Black Triggerfishes, form huge aggregations that include several hundred individuals. If fish bait is tossed on the surface where these fishes are present, their voracious feeding activity causes the surface to literally boil. The powerful jaws are used for feeding on a wide variety of items including sea urchins, starfishes, crabs, shrimps, and molluscs. Some species scrape filamentous algae from the surface of the reef. Triggerfishes of the genus *Xanthichthys* form schools that swim high above the bottom, usually in deeper water. They feed on planktonic food consisting largely of various copepods. The males of this genus are more brilliantly colored than the females.

Most triggerfishes do not exceed about 30 cm in length, but members of the genus *Pseudobalistes* reach a formidable size (to about 60 cm). *Pseudobalistes viridescens* deposits its eggs in a sandy depression excavated by the parents. After spawning, the eggs are closely guarded by the male, who vigorously chases away potential egg-eaters. In the Maldives we learned to give this species a wide berth after both of us received painful bites during filming activities. In one instance one of the authors (G.R.A.) warded off the attack of an agitated nest-guarding male by thrusting an aluminum camera housing at the charging trigger. To our surprise the fish seized the flash mounting arm in its jaws and swam off with the housing for a short distance before depositing it on the bottom.

Relatively few filefishes are seen on Indo-Pacific coral reefs. There are an estimated 30 species found in the tropical Indian Ocean, but the majority of these are either uncommon in reef areas or have their main distribution in sandy or weedy trawling grounds. Australia has more filefishes than any other area in the world, with 54 species known from the island continent. Over one-third of these, however, are inhabitants of the cooler temperate zone. Common coral reef genera include *Alutera, Amanses, Cantherhines, Paraluteres, Oxymonacanthus,* and *Pervagor.* However, most of these groups are represented by only one or two species. The most colorful of these is the Long-snout Filefish, *Oxymonacanthus longirostris,* which is most often encountered among the branches of *Acropora* coral.

# Chapter Thirty

# *Reproduction*

The large majority of reef fishes are open-water spawners. They release relatively large numbers of eggs, often several thousand per female, during a single spawning. These eggs are generally buoyant and float to the surface. A large percentage of the eggs are eaten by various fishes; for example, wrasses are notorious in this respect. The large number of eggs produced by open-water spawners provides some measure of insurance for the survival of at least a few eggs from each brood. The eggs generally hatch after one to five days, and the resultant larvae are then at the mercy of waves and currents to transport them to inshore reef areas. Some fishes, such as the surgeons (Acanthuridae), have extended larval stages that may last for several months. Therefore they may be transported hundreds or even thousands of miles before settling on a suitable reef. There is evidence indicating that some species with long larval stages have the capability of delaying metamorphosis to the juvenile stage for extensive periods if the larvae fail to drift into a suitable shallow habitat. The tiny larval stages of reef fishes are generally transparent or silvery in color and bear little resemblance to the colorful adult stages. When they are washed into shallow reefs a gradual metamorphosis or transformation occurs in which the bland larval colors give way to the more brilliant juvenile pattern.

Many open-water spawners exhibit a more or less stereotyped pattern of spawning behavior. It is characterized by male displays of rapid or erratic swimming, exaggerated pectoral fin movements, and erection of the dorsal and anal fins. These postures are often accompanied by bouts of chasing and biting directed at one or more females. The actual spawning sequence consists of a rapid burst of swimming at a sharp angle of up to several meters toward the surface. Gametes (eggs and sperm) are simultaneously released as the fish abruptly change direction and head for the bottom. This type of spawning is characteristic of wrasses, parrotfishes, butterflyfishes, angelfishes, boxfishes or cowfishes, and a host of other reef-dwellers.

In contrast to the open-water or pelagic spawners are the relatively few marine egglaying fishes that deposit their eggs on the bottom. Perhaps the best reef-dwelling examples in this category are the damselfishes (Pomacentridae). The males, sometimes with help from the female partner, laboriously prepare a nest site by repeatedly biting and removing algal growth, sessile invertebrates, and detritus. The pectoral fins are also utilized to fan away silt and debris. Courtship behavior involves much chasing and quick, erratic swimming. In addition, one or both partners assume an unusual nuptial coloration often very different from the normal livery. Damselfishes and other bottom-nesting groups generally exhibit some form of parental care. Consequently they have a higher percentage of hatching success compared with open water spawners and it is not necessary to produce prodigious numbers of eggs to ensure the survival of at least a few offspring. Thus the bottom-nesters usually have small clutches containing anywhere from about 50 to several hundred eggs. In the case of damselfishes, the male parent vigorously defends a territory centered around the nest site and drives away all potential egg predators, particularly wrasses of the genera *Thalassoma* and *Halichoeres*. The nest is usually situated on the underside of a rock, on the inner surface of a dead bivalve mollusc, on a small section of dead coral skeleton, on wreckage, or even inside a discarded tin can. Hatching occurs in two to seven days depending on the species, and the free-swimming larvae generally rise to the surface. At this stage they are abandoned by the parents and the subsequent life history is similar to that of the larvae of the open water spawners. Other bottom-spawning groups include the gobies, blennies, triplefins, and some triggerfishes.

A special category of bottom-spawning fishes includes species that brood their eggs in the oral cavity of one of the spawning partners, frequently the male. Several individual eggs or a gelatinous egg mass is taken up in the mouth where it remains until hatching, which may require several days to more than one week. During this period the brooding parent is unable to feed although eggs are sometimes ingested, apparently by accident. Mouthbrooding groups include cardinalfishes, ariid catfishes, and some members of the families Pseudochromidae and Plesiopidae.

Seahorses and pipefishes are characterized by a brood pouch on the ventral surface of the male. This structure is missing in some species, in which case the female deposits eggs directly on the surface of the male in a special region that is highly vascularized. The eggs thus develop under the care of the male, who gives birth after several weeks of "pregnancy." This is women's lib in the true sense of the word!

Very few marine fishes bear living young, but this mode of reproduction is found in a small number of reef groups such as sharks, rays, cusk eels (families Brotulidae and Bythitidae), and in the clinids, a family of small weed-dwelling fishes that are most common in southern Australia.

Hybridization, a relatively common phenomenon among freshwater species, is poorly documented in marine fishes. However, a small number of coral reef fish hybrids have been collected or photographed by divers in recent years. Most of these belong to the families Chaetodontidae, Pomacanthidae, and Acanthuridae. Crossbreeding usually occurs between an abundant species and a closely related congener that is locally rare.

# Chapter Thirty-one

# *Boxfishes and Puffers*

Because of their unusual appearance the boxfishes (Ostraciontidae) and puffers (Tetraodontidae and Diodontidae) are a conspicuous element of the reef fauna. These fishes belong to an assemblage known as the Plectognatha and are among the most advanced of all teleosts. They exhibit a number of specialized morphological features that include the absence of pelvic fins, a lack of spiny fin rays, and the possession of either a hard exterior covering or the ability to inflate their body to a size several times greater than normal. All are relatively sluggish, slow- moving animals that row through the water chiefly with their pectoral fins. Because of their hard body surface or ability to swell they are not considered a high priority item by most predators. These specializations tend to compensate for their lack of speed. The diet is an omnivorous one consisting of such items as algae, various crustaceans, polychaetes, sponges, corals (both hard and soft), tunicates, starfishes, sea urchins, sea cucumbers, and hard-shelled molluscs. The heavy teeth and strong jaws are particularly effective for crushing the last item.

There are less than 15 species of boxfishes inhabiting Indian Ocean reefs. Most belong to the genera *Ostracion* or *Lactoria*. The latter group are sometimes called cowfishes due to the possession of a pair of bony horns that project from the forehead. *Ostracion cubicus* and *O. meleagris* are the two most frequently encountered boxfishes on coral reefs. The young of the former species are bright yellow and very square-shaped. The unusual appearance of these fishes coupled with their poor swimming ability make them an easy target for novice aquarium fish collectors. Unfortunately, when these fishes are placed under stress they exude a toxic mucus that is capable of killing any fishes that happen to be in the same aquarium or collecting bucket. Experienced collectors are able to overcome this problem by vigorously shaking the fish in the open sea for several minutes until the supply of toxin has been depleted. Apparently it takes a relatively long period for the poison to build up to a dangerous level, by which time the fish can be successfully acclimated to life in captivity.

There are approximately 40 species of pufferfishes found in the Indian Ocean, but only about half of this total are encountered on coral reefs. About 10 Indian Ocean species belong to the porcupinefish family Diodontidae. They are equipped with sharp spikes that cover most of the body. Both porcupinefishes and the tetraodontid puffers can inflate themselves by swallowing water or air if out of water. Most reef puffers belong to either *Arothron* or *Canthigaster*. The latter group, known as sharpnose puffers, is represented on Indian Ocean reefs by 13 species. Their relatively small size (usually under 10 cm) and bright color patterns make them desirable aquarium pets.

# Chapter Thirty-Two

# *Miscellaneous Reef Fishes*

The major families of coral reef fishes were covered in the preceding chapters. There remains, however, a variety of smaller families and others that may be relatively large but not well represented on most reefs and some that contain species that are mainly cryptic in habit.

Sand, rubble, and weeds provide a home for a number of species, but because of their camouflage coloration coupled with the fact that most divers spend little time in these surroundings, they go largely unnoticed. Lizardfishes (Synodontidae), flatheads (Platycephalidae), and flatfishes (Bothidae, etc.) blend in extremely well with the sandy bottom, a characteristic used to full advantage in capturing small fishes that stray from the protective cover of adjacent reefs. Rubble and sand also offer a haven for the dragonets (Callionymidae), worm gobies (Microdesmidae), and sand tilefishes (Branchiostegidae). The first named are small to medium sized fishes that comb the bottom in search of tiny crustaceans. The latter two families contain only a small number of species that typically swim in midwater with an undulating movement. In the face of danger they retreat to burrows on the bottom. Sand divers (Trichonotidae), another sand-dwelling family, typically plunge headlong under the sandy substratum when threatened. They remain buried for long periods but keep a lookout for danger by thrusting their eyes above the surface of the sand. Males possess delicate prolonged filaments that are prominently displayed during courtship. The plotosid catfishes (Plotosidae) inhabit weed, rubble, and reef areas. Juveniles sometimes form huge aggregations that raise a big cloud of dusty silt during their foraging activities. These fishes possess venomous fin spines and must therefore be carefully handled. The silver biddies or mojarras (Gerreidae) are nondescript fishes often seen in shallow bays with silt or sand bottoms. They are sometimes caught in large quantities by commercial net fishermen. The guitarfishes (Rhinobatidae) are a type of ray that often grows to a length of 2-3 meters. They are occasionally seen lying on sand or silt bottoms adjacent to reef areas.

Among the most interesting of the cryptic reef dwellers are the anglerfishes (Antennariidae). The first dorsal spine is specially modified to form a thin rod that is equipped with a filamentous "bait" at the tip. The bait is often in the shape of a small worm, octopus, or other invertebrate and is most effective in luring small fishes within range of the cavernous mouth of this voracious predator. The deep fissures and ledges of the reef provide a home for the cusk eels (Bythitidae) and clingfishes (Gobiesocidae). Some members of the latter family form symbiotic associations with sea lilies (crinoids) and urchins. More obvious dwellers of caverns include the sweeps or bullseyes (Pempheridae) and the southern Australian swallowtail, *Trachichthodes lineatus* (Berycidae).

The trumpetfish *Aulostomus chinensis* (Aulostomidae) is a clever hunter of small fishes. It sometimes sneaks up on unsuspecting prey by concealing itself behind larger species such as goatfishes or parrotfishes. It will travel long distances swimming close beside the larger fish until the opportunity to strike arises. The remora or shark-sucker *Echeneis naucrates* (Echeneidae) is well known for its habit of hitching a ride on the surface of sharks, rays, whales, and turtles. Its unique sucking disc represents a modification of the dorsal fin. The weed whitings (Odacidae) make up a small family found on weed-covered reefs of southern Australia and New Zealand. They are close relatives of the wrasses but have fused teeth in the jaws that are similar to those of parrotfishes.

## Chapter Thirty-three

# *Reef Oddities*

Coral reefs provide refuge for an astonishing variety of fishes. They range in size from tiny gobies of 1-2 cm to leviathans such as the whale shark, which although mainly an inhabitant of the open sea is occasionally seen near reefs. The array of shapes and colors exhibited by coral reef fishes seems almost endless. Equally fascinating is the bewildering variety of behavioral regimes, feeding strategies, and ecological roles that are displayed. This final grouping of oddities is reflected in the illustrations that depict either uncommon and bizarre species of fishes that, although abundant, have peculiar morphological features or behavior patterns that frequently arouse the curiosity of underwater observers.

# References

There are very few comprehensive reference works available that treat Indian Ocean fishes. Several major works including those of Day, Klunzinger, Playfair, Rueppell, and Sauvage were published over 100 years ago but are still much utilized by ichthyologists. Perhaps the single most valuable reference work currently available is J. L. B. Smith's *Sea Fishes of Southern Africa*, which has been reprinted several times since the first edition. A completely revised and up to date version of this valuable work is currently in preparation under the direction of the late Prof. Smith's wife, Margaret M. Smith.

There are numerous technical articles treating Indian Ocean fishes that appear in various scientific journals. However, these are useful primarily to professional taxonomists. In the list of references below we include only a few of the major comprehensive reference books. The older titles are available only at the larger libraries of major cities or in the libraries of universities, museums, or other scientific institutions that keep permanent fish collections. Most of the recent titles are still available from either the publisher or book dealers who specialize in biological titles.

ALLEN, G. R. and R. C. STEENE. 1979. The fishes of Christmas Island, Indian Ocean. *Spec. Publ. 2*. Austral. Nat. Parks Wildlife Serv., Canberra. 81 pp., 15 pls.

BOCK, K. 1978. *A Guide to Common Reef Fishes of the Western Indian Ocean*. Macmillan, London. 122 pp., 16 pls.

BURGESS, W. E. and H. R. AXELROD. 1973. *Fishes of Sri Lanka, the Maldive Islands, and Mombasa. Pacific Marine Fishes Book 3*. T.F.H. Publ. Inc., 272 pp., 343 col. photos.

DAY, F. 1875-78. *The fishes of India; being a natural history of fishes known to inhabit the seas and freshwaters of India, Burma, and Ceylon*. London. xx, 778 pp., 198 pls.

JONES, S. and M. KUMARAN. 1980. *Fishes of the Laccadive Archipelago*. Mathrubhumi Press, Cochin. 700 pp.

KLUNZINGER, C. B. 1870-71. Synopsis der Fische des Rothen Meeres. I & II Theil. *Verh. Zool.-Bot. Ges. Wien*, 20: 669-834; 21: 441-668.

KURONUMA, K. and Y. ABE. 1972. *Fishes of Kuwait*. Kuwait Inst. Sci. Res. 123 pp., 20 pls.

KYUSHIN, K., K. AMAOKA, K. NAKAYA, and H. IDA. 1977. *Fishes of the Indian Ocean*. Japan. Mar. Fish. Resource Res. Cen. 392 pp., 179 pls.

MUNRO, I. S. R. 1955. *The marine and freshwater fishes of Ceylon*. Dept. Ext. Affairs (Australia), Canberra. 351 pp., 56 pls.

PLAYFAIR, R. L. and A. GUENTHER. 1866. *The fishes of Zanzibar, with a list of the fishes of the whole east coast of Africa*. London. 156 pp.

RANDALL, J.E., G.R. ALLEN, and W.F. SMITH-VANIZ. 1978. *Illustrated identification guide to commercial fishes (of the Persian Gulf)*. FAO, Rome. 221 pp., numerous pls.

RUEPPELL, W. 1826. *Atlas zu der Reise im nordlichen Afrika. Zoologie, Fische des Rothen Meeres*. 4 vols. Frankfurt-a-M. 119 pls.

SAUVAGE, H. E. 1875. Vol. 16 - Poissons. in: Grandier, A., *Histoire physique, naturelle et politique de Madagascar*. Paris. 543 pp., 61 pls.

SMITH, J. L. B. 1949. *The sea fishes of Southern Africa*. Central News Agency. 559 pp., 102 pls., 1232 figs.

SMITH, J. L. B. 1956-1961. *Ichthyological Bulletins 1-32*. M. M. Smith ed. (Vol. 1, Bulls. 1-20, reprinted 1969; Vol. 2, Bulls. 21-32, reprinted 1973.) J. L. B. Smith Inst. Ichthyol., Rhodes Univ., Grahamstown, South Africa.

SMITH, J. L. B. and M. M. SMITH. 1963. *The fishes of Seychelles*. Dept. Ichthyol., Rhodes Univ., Grahamstown, South Africa. 215 pp., 98 pls.

SMITH, M. M. 1975. *Common and scientific names of the fishes of Southern Africa*. Part I. Marine Fishes. *Spec. Publ.*, No. 14. J.L.B. Smith Inst. Ichthyol., Rhodes Univ., Grahamstown, South Africa. 213 pp.

# GENERAL INDEX

# ILLUSTRATIONS INDEX

This index is to the color photos of the plate section of this book. The number before the hyphen is the plate number, that after the hyphen refers to the photo number on the plate.